Pluralism

DATE OF RETURN
UNLESS RECALLED BY LIBRARY

PLEASE TAKE GOOD CARE OF THIS BOOK

Pluralism

PETER LASSMAN

polity

First published in 2011 by Polity Press

Polity Press
65 Bridge Street
Cambridge CB2 1UR, UK

Polity Press
350 Main Street
Malden, MA 02148, USA

ISBN-13: 978-0-7456-1617-9
ISBN-13: 978-0-7456-1618-6(pb)

A catalogue record for this book is available from the British Library.

Typeset in 11 on 13 pt Berling
by Toppan Best-set Premedia Limited
Printed and bound in Great Britain by MPG Books Group Limited,
Bodmin, Cornwall

For further information on Polity, visit our website: www.politybooks.com

Contents

Acknowledgements

Writing this book took much longer than I, or probably anyone else, expected. Along the way I learned much from discussions with colleagues in the Theory Group of the Department of Political Science and International Studies of the University of Birmingham. Steve Buckler, Jethro Butler, Cecile Hatier, Jeremy Jennings, Jamie Reed, Richard North, Alan Shadforth and Richard Shorten were all long-standing participants. I must also thank the two Richards for putting up with my continual and uninvited interruptions to their working day. I, of course, take full responsibility for all the shortcomings and deficiencies on display here. Despite the destructive policies that have resulted from the occupation of English universities by the forces of a philistine and crude form of utilitarian managerialism, I remain firm in my, perhaps, utopian conviction that the study of political theory can continue to operate as a form of intellectual resistance.

Some of the material here appeared in an earlier form in *Critical Review of International Social and Political Philosophy*, *Etica e Politica*, *History of Political Thought*, and *Max Weber Studies*.

Special thanks go to Sue, Daniel, Amy, Ellen, Sue, Nathan, Mila and Ruby.

1
Pluralism

1 The Problem

The problem of value pluralism is a central topic in modern political theory. Its presence is discernible even when, at first sight, its significance is not immediately apparent. There are two important questions here. The first is to ask what kind of problem it is. The second is to inquire why it is that political theorists have come to think of it as a problem. In answering these questions, we have to recognize that there is some ambiguity regarding the way in which the term 'value pluralism' has come to be used. Pluralism can be understood either as a description of one aspect of the social condition of modern western societies or as a controversial philosophical thesis about the nature of value. If it is defined as the latter it is a philosophical theory that does, many would argue, have political implications. It is also a fact, as Bernard Williams has pointed out, that the modern world has become particularly conscious of value pluralism in both senses.[1]

The idea of 'pluralism' has become so pervasive that, for example, according to Richard Flathman, almost every modern political theorist seems to be a pluralist. He sees the core of pluralism in a broad sense as 'the recognition of a multiplicity of persons and groups . . . A commitment to pluralism, however transitory or transitional, as a descriptive/analytic theory involves the belief that, here and now, such a multiplicity cannot be explained away'.[2] In his discussion of pluralism, Flathman admits that although most are pluralists to some degree, for others it is a superficial and trivial idea that conceals the deeper truth of its opposite, monism. Of course, there are many different things other than values about which one can take a pluralist attitude.

Although the concept of pluralism can be used in this rather general manner, the most significant and puzzling form of pluralism that concerns modern political theorists is the version generally known as 'value pluralism'. The debate about value pluralism has become increasingly complex. Unfortunately, there is often a lack of clarity both about the claims made and their implications. First, it is not always clear what philosophers and political theorists mean when they talk about 'values'. For example, one could point to a distinction that is frequently made in discussions of the pluralism of moral values, between a view that sees value as residing in goods or ends, while others see value in terms of rules and principles.[3] However, despite what is often a lack of conceptual clarity in the political literature, the point of these discussions is usually fairly clear. Most discussions of value pluralism among political theorists take a view of value in terms of the realization of public goods, such as liberty, equality, or justice.

Not everyone is happy with the kind of talk about values that pervades much modern political thought. For instance, some theorists working within a broadly Aristotelian tradition argue that its generally accepted vocabulary – in which concepts of rights, autonomy, and value pluralism play a central role – is deeply deficient. They argue that the modern language of 'values' and, therefore, of value pluralism is itself 'a pathological feature of modern moral experience'. All talk of 'values' is regarded as unnecessarily subjective. The language of plural values underwritten by a fear of a monism of values, it is argued, functions to rule out any constructive consideration of the question of a strong sense of the human good that is a presupposition of all political theories.[4] It is true that much neo-Aristotelian theory does present an important and powerful antidote to many of the assumptions of the predominantly liberal forms of modern Anglo-American theory. It is also true that not all who work within a broadly conceived Aristotelian tradition are completely hostile to the idea of value pluralism.

Although they accept the truth of value pluralism, they do not accept the conclusions that are drawn from it by liberal political philosophers often inspired by Kant.[5] However, for the moment, it is probably sufficient to agree that in ordinary usage, for better or worse, the language of values used is generally intelligible without it necessarily having the pathological and subjective implications for which it has been charged.[6]

It is also worth mentioning how strange it is that the language of 'values' has slipped so easily into modern philosophy and political theory. It seems that 'value' as a philosophical concept was initially borrowed from the language of political economy in Germany during the first half of the nineteenth century. The turning point, it is generally recognized, was Nietzsche's idea of 'the revaluation of values'. It must be noted, too, that Nietzsche's account of values is deeply sceptical of the 'metaphysical faith' in the existence of 'antithetical values'.[7] Nevertheless, the concept of 'value' was further developed in debates in the early twentieth century concerning the nature of the differences between the natural and the human sciences. Max Weber, Wilhelm Dilthey, Heinrich Rickert and other neo-Kantian philosophers were prominent figures in these debates. All were deeply worried by the problem of the objectivity of value, the plurality of values, and the relationship between 'fact' and 'value'. Never far away in all of these debates is the question of nihilism raised so dramatically by Nietzsche.[8] Of course, not everyone during this period was happy with the idea of a philosophy of value. Notably, Heidegger objected to what he saw as its triviality, while Carl Schmitt, with similar concerns, felt the need to condemn what he regarded as 'the tyranny of values'.[9] In a similar vein, Hannah Arendt interpreted the modern obsession with values as a symptom of the intellectual and political confusion brought about by the overturning of the western political and philosophical tradition that, in her view, began with Plato and ended with Marx.[10]

Discussion of the question of value pluralism and the related question of disagreement has become prominent for many reasons. Among them is the enduring search for an adequate understanding of the nature of politics and of political knowledge. This alone places the problem of pluralism at the centre of political theory. It has been argued that, as value pluralism is a philosophical thesis, 'it does more than record the fact that choice often involves conflicts, moral and other, and that choosing can be a difficult and sometimes appalling thing to do'.[11] The claims made on behalf of value pluralism are meant to be more challenging. For example, one of the central arguments made by strong value pluralists is the view that values are not simply plural. The key point for the political theorist is that they are often in conflict. Furthermore, the worry here is that cases of value conflict are often strongly resistant to clear-cut or rational resolution. Linked to this is the idea that situations of value conflict sometimes present us with dilemmas where regret will be the result of whatever outcome we choose. Clearly, if this is so, then the implications for the practice of politics are great and wide-ranging.

There are clearly two aspects that have to be distinguished. Value pluralism can be seen as an empirical fact about the world that refers, for example, to the reality of cultural difference and diversity. However, more interestingly and controversially, value pluralism can be seen as a theory about the nature of value. Of course, if the theory of value pluralism is true, it is stating a significant fact about the world. Furthermore, the theory of pluralism cannot itself escape from being an object of controversy and disagreement – the theory is open to a plurality of conflicting interpretations. If pluralism is correct as a theory about value, then we ought to expect pluralism about pluralism. The theory of value pluralism is a complex philosophical idea and our attitude to it can have important implications for the way in which we think we are able or ought to understand the political world.

Political philosophers who put forward the idea of value pluralism generally tend to think of it primarily in either epistemic or metaphysical terms. For instance, if value pluralism implies the intractability of disagreements in moral and political affairs, then taken from an epistemic point of view these disagreements imply that they are a product of the limitations of human reason. This, it can be argued, is simply a fact that we just have to accept and learn to live with. Given the complexity of many of the moral and political problems we face, it is often argued that human reason is unable to provide a clear decision procedure when confronted with the reality of choices between what are often equally valid alternatives. On the other hand, a more metaphysical or ontological account of value pluralism argues that it is not so much the weakness or limitations of human reason that constitute the problem. We have to recognize it just is a fact that it is the values themselves that are plural and that they often are in conflict with each other. One politically relevant implication of this view is that, if the universe is structured in this way, then there is no optimal way in which all goods can be either ranked or realized equally. One of the political implications of this message is often taken to be a warning against what are deemed to be the dangers that are bound to result from utopian and, by implication, impossible attempts to create a harmony of values on earth.[12]

It is sometimes argued that value pluralism is a relatively new idea. According to this account, most of the thinkers who make up the canon of western political thought were monists in their understanding of the nature of values. Isaiah Berlin has been the most influential proponent and, probably, originator, of this view. It appears that monism has gone out of fashion, to a large degree, although there are some notable defenders of the monistic point of view. It is also true to say that in the eyes of many theorists the arguments for pluralism, when subjected to rigorous analysis, become unclear and inconclusive. On close inspection, what has been referred to as a 'value pluralist movement' in political philosophy does not refer to the proposition of a clearly defined theory about values but instead to a set of overlapping concerns about the nature of the world of modern politics and the problem of how best to make sense of it. Rather than looking for a conclusive definition of pluralism, drawn from the ways in which it is generally understood by political theorists, it probably makes more sense to regard non-reductive value pluralism as 'a convenient rubric under which a loose collection of different views about values may be grouped'.[13] The approach taken here, rather than discussing whether value pluralism as a philosophical theory is true or false, is to ask what the idea means and the purpose that it has served in the work of some of those modern political thinkers who have taken it to be a serious problem.

It is clear that the discussion of pluralism among political theorists reveals a range of overlapping ideas and concerns. It would be a mistake to assume that all who talk about pluralism necessarily share an identical understanding of the nature of the problems that it generates. For example, it would be wrong to deny that there is a common concern in the philosophical literature with the problems of incommensurability and incomparability. However, when these questions have been taken up by political theorists, they have, in turn, seen their theoretical significance to lie more in such problems as the nature and sources of political conflict and disagreement, the question of stability in liberal states, the defence of liberalism under modern conditions, and, ultimately, of our understanding of politics, 'the political', and the role of reason in politics, rather than in questions about the nature of value as such. Following a suggestion made by Isaiah Berlin, adapted from Bertrand Russell, it is instructive to bear in mind an idea of 'the inner citadel'. This term refers to the basic problem or set of problems, often unstated, that lie at the heart of any political philosophy. According to Berlin:

> the deepest convictions of philosophers are seldom contained in their formal arguments: fundamental beliefs, comprehensive views of life, are like citadels which must be guarded against the enemy. Philosophers expend their intellectual power in arguments against actual and possible objections to their doctrines, and although the reasons they find, and the logic that they use, may be complex, ingenious and formidable, they are defensive weapons; the inner fortress itself – the vision of life for the sake of which the war is being waged – will, as a rule, turn out to be relatively simple and unsophisticated.[14]

For example, in the case of Berlin himself it is clear that whatever the philosophical questions that might have originally sparked his awareness of the problem of pluralism, the enormous importance that he came to attach to it was fuelled by his opposition to totalitarianism, which he regarded as a particularly dangerous form of utopian monism. This, in turn, was an integral part of his defence of liberalism. This is a clear example of the way in which use of the concept of pluralism takes on its meaning and significance in the work of a political philosopher in terms of its relationship to the 'inner citadel' of basic worries and concerns.

Nevertheless, it has almost become a commonplace to claim that a 'value-pluralist movement' has emerged in modern political theory. This 'movement' owes a clear debt to Berlin's work.[15] The most prominent members of this so-called movement usually include, among others, Bernard Williams, Stuart Hampshire, Joseph Raz, Steven Lukes, Thomas Nagel, Charles Taylor, Charles Larmore and John Gray. Despite the differences between them, it is clear that one thing they do have in common is a belief that recognition of the plurality of values, both as a fact and as a theory about the modern world, presents political thinking with a distinct and new set of problems.

It is generally agreed that the origin of this concern with pluralism in modern Anglo-American political philosophy, at least, is to be found in the work of Isaiah Berlin. All of the philosophers and political theorists mentioned above refer to a greater or lesser degree to Berlin's work, although they do not always agree about how it is best understood or the conclusions that we ought to draw from it. The renewal of interest in the work of Berlin is itself an interesting, intriguing and controversial development in modern political thought. In fact, the revival of interest in Berlin's intellectual legacy has to a large extent been bound up with the idea that the problem of pluralism is both a central problem for modern political thought and that it is the unifying theme in his work (or, at least, one of the unifying themes).

The original source of the modern value-pluralist movement for political theorists, it is generally claimed, can be found in Berlin's famous lecture 'Two Concepts of Liberty' and, in particular, in its concluding section which has the title of the 'The One and the Many'.[16] Berlin concluded his reflections on the relative merits of what he famously called 'positive' and 'negative' liberty by revealing the underlying premises of his argument. It is here that he states in a very forceful way the idea that it is our fate to live in a world where we are confronted with a plurality of values, often incommensurable, but certainly in 'perpetual rivalry'. Berlin makes his understanding of the importance of this idea even clearer when, on the first page of his lecture, he states that, if there were no discord or conflict about ultimate purposes, then there would be no need for politics and, therefore, nothing, strictly speaking, for political theorists to talk about. Indeed, Berlin pointed out that much of the contemporary academic study of politics conducted by social scientists and philosophers seemed to be carried on as if there were no such deep disagreements about political ideas. Considering the fact that Berlin was writing during the time

of intense ideological and political struggle that is known as
'the Cold War', this is an even more remarkable fact. It is also
a reflection of the detachment from politics that the intellectual style of much contemporary academic political theorizing
still seems to encourage. For Berlin, it is clear that the study
of politics is both made possible by and thrives on the disagreements that are, in his view, produced by the pluralism of values.

After Berlin, the most influential account of pluralism as a
problem for political theory has been that put forward by John
Rawls. This is not to deny that the theme of value pluralism
was also present in the work of many other theorists writing
during this period. Political thinkers such as Raymond Aron,
Friedrich von Hayek and Karl Popper all subscribed to versions
of the view that an appreciation of the reality of plural and
conflicting values was an essential component of an adequate
understanding of modern politics. Nevertheless, it is John
Rawls who made it a central feature of his theory of political
liberalism that it must be able to face up to what he terms 'the
fact of pluralism'. What Rawls means by this is that the diversity of what he calls 'comprehensive doctrines' is a permanent
feature of the political life of modern democracies. As he puts
it: 'the fact about free institutions is the fact of pluralism'.[17]

In fact, it is interesting that Rawls refers to two precursors
in the history of political theory who have also made the
problem of the pluralism of values central for their thought.
He argues that the fact that both Isaiah Berlin and Max Weber
stand out as political thinkers in the modern age is due to their
appreciation of the centrality and relevance of the challenge of
plural and conflicting values for both political life and political
theory. Rawls has called upon Berlin's account of pluralism in
support of his own idea of political liberalism. For example, he
agrees with Berlin's idea that in any complex political society
some ways of life that instantiate certain fundamental values
are bound to be excluded as the price to be paid for realization
of others.[18] Rawls, however, implies but does not elaborate
upon the differences in the way that he, Weber and Berlin
understand the problem of pluralism.

What are the main claims made by the political theorists of
pluralism? The central claims made by most pluralists have
been conveniently summarized by William Galston. Arguing
for a form of liberal pluralism that is closely related to Isaiah

Berlin's account of value pluralism, Galston puts forward the following basic points (although not in this order).

1. Values or objective goods cannot be fully rank-ordered. 'This means that there is no common measure for all goods, which are qualitatively heterogeneous. It means that there is no summum bonum that is the chief good for all individuals. It means that there are no comprehensive lexical orderings among types of goods'.
2. Value pluralism ought not to be confused with relativism.
3. Value pluralists are prepared to recognize that it is possible to defend an account of those goods that are required for any 'choiceworthy conception of human life'.
4. Beyond this there is a wide range of goods. These are all legitimate and open to free choice and deliberation.
5. Value pluralism as a theory is to be distinguished from its opposite: monism. In Galston's definition, a theory of value is monistic if it attempts to reduce all goods to a common measure or to create a comprehensive hierarchy or ordering for them.[19]

Similarly, Bernard Williams has argued for the recognition of the moral and political significance of the 'plural, conflicting and irreducible' nature of values. Pluralists such as Berlin and Williams 'regard the conflicts as both ineliminable and not resoluble without remainder'.[20] Furthermore, an important point that pluralists such as Berlin and Williams are keen to make is that they do not think it is right to regard value conflict as a pathology that needs to or that can be overcome, either by theorizing or as the result of the unfolding of some historical process. The acceptance of the idea that the existence of plural and conflicting values is a symptom of a deeper confusion or lack of understanding has found expression in both an analytical philosophical and in a Hegelian and Marxist version. For Williams, claiming that values are incommensurable is to say four 'true and important things'. In order of the increasing strength of these claims: (i) there is no currency in terms of which each conflict of values can be resolved; (ii) it is not true that for each conflict of values there is some independent value which can be appealed to in order to resolve that conflict; (iii) there is no independent value that can be appealed to in order to rationally resolve that conflict; and (iv) no conflict of values can ever be rationally resolved. Even if the last proposition claims too much for the thesis of value pluralism as incommensurabilty, the other three claims are significant enough to create problems for the political theorist.

One other aspect of the defence of the thesis of pluralism has to be mentioned, as it clearly animates much of the reflection of many political thinkers. This is the way in which taking pluralism seriously as a problem is linked with the rejection of 'utopianism'. This can take two forms. The first is a rejection of the notion that conflicts of value are reducible to the ideological conflicts characteristic of a certain stage of social development. According to this view, such conflicts of value are not permanent features of social and political life and can be therefore be overcome as a result of radical transformation. The other form of utopianism is represented by the desire to construct a systematic ethical and political theory that would have the power to reduce or remove conflicts and uncertainties.[21]

Strong pluralists generally deny the possibility and the desirability of any attempts to produce a rational ordering or ranking of values. The problem for political theory, if this proposition is accepted, becomes one of deciding what the appropriate response ought to be. It is important to be clear that it is not the philosophical question of the reality of diverse sources of value that is primarily the problem here. Rather, it is the idea of the inescapability of plural and conflicting values and the resulting persistence of disagreement that has troubled political theorists. Clearly, not all disagreement need be thought of as the product of value pluralism. The fact of pervasive disagreement is not inconsistent with a monistic theory of value. For example, pervasive conflict and disagreement could be generated by competing interpretations of different aspects of a single value. Nevertheless, what Rawls has called 'the fact of pluralism' has come to be thought of as one of a main, if not the main, source of political disagreement in the modern world.[22] It would seem that the basic problem of value pluralism for political theorists is not so much their plurality, but the implication of their supposed incommensurability and incomparability. These two properties are, in turn, held to be responsible for the persistence of disagreement. The persistence of disagreement is one of the fundamental and 'inconvenient' stubborn facts of politics.

2 Disagreement

Although it is often argued that a distinction ought to be made between pluralism and disagreement, it has become increasingly clear that one of the key problems that has emerged, for political theorists, from the debate about pluralism is that of the persistence of intractable political disagreement. In this sense, recognition of the problem of disagreement as a stubborn and 'inconvenient' fact, in Max Weber's sense, leads us back to what is one of the fundamental questions about the nature of politics. We can call this 'the fact or circumstance of politics'.[23] In modern political thought, for instance, it is possible to discern in the contemplation of this fact a deep rift between a distinctly 'Kantian' strand which, ultimately, puts its faith in a particular concept of reason, and a more 'Nietzschean' strand that is sceptical of the claims of reason in politics.[24] In fact, the tension between these two tendencies can often be a creative force, not only between different theorists but also within the work of a single theorist. It can be argued, for example, that it is the presence of this tension in Max Weber's attempt to come to terms with 'the war of the gods' that enables his work to transcend its immediate historical location and to retain its interest.

Although it is possible to imagine deep disagreements within a monistic world of value, it is those disagreements thought to be generated by the existence of plural and conflicting values that have most concerned contemporary political thinkers. Some see this as an important development that tells us something new and significant about the modern world. Others see it as a necessary corrective to some of the dominant tendencies in modern political thinking. It is often argued that both the experience of value pluralism and the deeper recognition of pervasive disagreement are a distinguishing feature of political modernity. At the same time, although it is true that we can trace the modern origins of these concerns, it can also be argued that they have a much longer history, if only in the shadows, of political thought from its ancient origins.[25] It is probably correct to say that not all political disagreement is necessarily the result of value pluralism and that the presence of disagreement does not necessarily entail the truth or existence of value pluralism. However, it would also seem correct to think that there is a close relationship between the presence of plural and conflicting values and the persistence of political disagreement. Or, perhaps, this is to get things the wrong way round. Value pluralism is not a necessarily given 'fact', but is, rather, as much the outcome of pervasive disagreement as it its precondition.

As a necessary corrective to the style of much contemporary political theorizing, Jeremy Waldron has proposed a distinction between theorizing about particular substantive political issues, such as the meaning of justice or rights, and general theorizing about the nature of politics.[26] He argues that there is a strong case to be made for redirecting our attention towards the overlooked and important problem of considering those ideas and concepts that are generally presupposed in theorizing about particular political issues. If we accept this argument, then it is clear that those questions normally associated with the problem of value pluralism ought to be of central importance for any theorizing about the nature of politics and 'the political'.

While the idea of value pluralism remains a philosophically controversial idea, political theorists have found their attention has been drawn increasingly to one aspect of it that is clearly of central significance for any account of the political domain. This is the reality of persistent disagreement. The focus on value pluralism and persistent disagreement is understood here as a more fundamental and troubling problem than the relatively uncontroversial fact of the existence of social and cultural pluralism. Fundamentally, the focus on pluralism and disagreement has produced the more radical thought that when it comes to many political and moral issues of central importance, reason is more likely to divide us than to bring us together.[27] Even in the case of what some theorists call 'reasonable pluralism' and 'reasonable disagreement', the basic and worrying idea is that 'reasonableness has ceased to offer, for many, a guarantee of ultimate agreement about deep questions concerning how we should live'.[28]

Examples of the concern with value pluralism can be cited from across the spectrum of theoretical and ideological standpoints. It would not be too much of an exaggeration to say that most contemporary political philosophy has to a large degree defined itself in terms of a need to respond to what is perceived as the problem of value pluralism. The problem, it would seem, for political theory is not so much that values might be plural, but, rather, that plural values can and do conflict with each other. It can be argued that this is confusion: that value pluralism, value conflict and persistent disagreement are separate and distinct topics. Although there is some truth in this, it is clear that what political thinkers have generally found challenging is not so much the question of the philosophical status of the arguments for and against pluralism as a theory of value, but that of formulating a convincing response to the reality of conflicting values. In other words, in political theory, pluralism and disagreement have generally been considered together.

3 Modernity and Disenchantment

The presence of value pluralism is often thought of as being a distinctly modern problem. For instance, an interesting example of this modern concern with value pluralism can be seen in the work of Alasdair MacIntyre. Although he is concerned primarily with questions of moral theory, his remarks have clear political implications. MacIntyre argues that:

> The most striking feature of contemporary moral utterance is that so much of it is used to express disagreements; and the most striking feature of the debates in which these disagreements are expressed is their interminable character. I do not mean by this just that such debates go on and on and on – although they do – but also that they can find no terminus. There seems to be no rational way of securing moral agreement in our culture.[29]

This statement is indicative of much that troubles those who take moral and value pluralism to be a definitive and troubling characteristic of the modern world. Of course, there is a range of possible attitudes that could be taken to this statement. One could deny the reality of value pluralism. Or, as does MacIntyre, one could accept its importance but resist its presumed inevitability. Others might draw more radical conclusions. For example, it is possible to accept that moral or value pluralism is a fact whose existence has serious implications for the scope of political theory and for the practice of politics itself. Indeed, one could argue that the consequences of pluralism, as understood in its modern sense, are such that one understanding of the traditional vocation of political theory as the search for a rational foundation for political practice is either undermined, or, at least, is seriously weakened. Of course, it is also possible to be sceptical and deny there is a genuine problem at all; it can be argued that upon deeper analysis value pluralism ceases to be the unsettling doctrine that many have taken it to be. Perhaps there is no genuine problem of pluralism. Either, if it is a problem, we are not really clear what sort of a problem it is, or, if there is a problem, then there is nothing radically new about it.[30]

Many would say that the existence and the persistence of moral and value pluralism is a vital condition for the possibility of politics. Nevertheless, it can be argued there is a sense in which, although the existence of plural and conflicting values is not as new a phenomenon as it is often claimed to be, there is, nevertheless, a peculiarly modern aspect to the recognition of the existence of pluralism as a problem for political theory. Increasingly, the idea that the modern world is characterized or, even more strongly, constituted by the existence of an unavoidable pluralism of conflicting values has itself become a central component of our own self-understanding. The idea of value pluralism becomes, in a sense, self-validating.

The awareness of the problem of pluralism is frequently related, even if implicitly, to some fundamental perceptions concerning the direction of modern western culture. It is often claimed, for instance, that the theory and practice of value pluralism is a reflection of the 'disenchanted world' of modernity in which we no longer believe that 'the aim of political association must be to bring man into harmony with God's purposes or to serve some comprehensive vision of the good life'.[31] Value pluralism is the inevitable result of the decline of the authority of political theology. Furthermore, it is argued that there is a close connection between liberalism and plural-

ism: both are related to 'the metaphysical-religious disenchantment of the world'.[32] It would appear that a historical
interpretation of the rationalization, secularization and progressive disenchantment of western society, such as that
advanced by Max Weber, supplies the often unacknowledged
background to much of the discussion of modern politics in a
world of value pluralism. Political theories of this kind tend to
rely upon the persuasive power of a narrative, often implicit,
that purports to explain how we have arrived at our current
situation. Such historical accounts or 'genealogies' become an
essential part of the supporting intellectual background argument for the theory.

The main relevant characteristic of the modern disenchanted
world is generally taken to be the loss or decline in our commitment to ultimate and authoritative frameworks of belief.
This means, of course, the decline in the authority of religious
belief, and the 'death of God'. Disenchanted modernity presents
us with

> a fundamentally different existential predicament from that
> which dominated most previous cultures and still defines the
> lives of other people today. That alternative is a predicament
> in which an unchallenged framework makes imperious demands
> which we fear being unable to meet . . . The form of the danger
> here is utterly different from that which threatens the modern
> seeker, which is something close to the opposite: the world
> loses altogether its spiritual contour, nothing is worth doing,
> the fear is of a terrifying emptiness, a kind of vertigo, or even
> a fracturing of our world and body-space.[33]

Disenchanted modernity, it is argued, has presented us with
two new and unexpected problems to cope with. A general
decline in the authority of moral and political judgements is
now combined with a general lack of coherence in our moral
ideas and the political beliefs that draw support from them. If
we accept this description as being reasonably accurate, even
if a little overdone rhetorically, it does point to the fact that
modern political theorists do operate in a markedly different
world to that of their predecessors and others who work within
the closed horizon of an unquestioned framework. Even if we
want to take a more detached and sceptical view of the dangers

of disenchantment, we cannot avoid recognizing the novelty of
the situation. It seems that:

> at best, we may have certainty within ourselves, but this cer-
> tainty is constantly jeopardized by the knowledge that others
> do not share it. There is no unquestionable framework even for
> those who do not, as a matter of fact, question the framework
> they adopt. Nor is there any obvious way of reconciling the
> different demands made by different frameworks.[34]

The problem that this raises for political theory and the justification of political ideas is daunting.

It is not too surprising that the problem of pluralism has
been taken by many as one of the, if not the, central problems
of political modernity. It is an often remarked upon fact that
so much of this debate has taken place within the boundaries
of liberal political theory. One reason for this is clear. Liberalism
in a broad sense is the form of modern political philosophy that
most directly seems to be both founded upon, to a large degree,
both the experience of the plurality and conflict of values, at
first mainly of religious origin, while, at the same time, seeing
the production of a satisfactory account of its own relation to
those competing values to be one of its greatest challenges.
However, it ought not to be thought that value pluralism has
been recognized as a problem only within the narrow confines
of a predominantly liberal form of Anglo-American political
theory. Generally misleading and unhelpful distinctions
between so-called 'continental' and 'Anglo-American' political
thought tend to hide the fact that pluralism, as the examples
of Max Weber and Nietzsche demonstrate, has been an important topic on both sides of the English Channel for some time.[35]

Furthermore, it can be argued that the significance of the
idea of pluralism rests on the role it plays in drawing our attention to the way in which 'fundamental divergences among
individuals' conceptions of the good present the distinctive
problems of modern politics, going beyond simple conflicts of
values'.[36] Following this suggestion, it is possible to clarify this
idea by pointing to three distinct levels in the analysis of plural
and conflicting values. For instance, Richardson argues that the
real problem arises from the 'phenomena of deep disagreement'. To make this idea clearer, he distinguishes between the

first case where values are similar but incompatible, a second where there is explicit disagreement over final ends, and a third where there is a clash between 'entire conceptions of value'. It is conflicts of this kind, he argues, that lead to the distinct problems of modern politics. An example of this kind of conflict is presented by the religious wars of seventeenth-century Europe. Here, religions aimed at different final ends, and provided 'contrasting models of reasoning, dissimilar concrete exemplars of virtue, and differing sets of propositions regarded as unquestionable'.[37] Clearly, there is an important distinction here, and Richardson is right to warn against conflating these different levels. It is important, too, not to think in terms of value pluralism as a clash of capital-letter abstractions such as LIBERTY and EQUALITY. In politics it is not the values as such that clash, but rather it is their instantiation in particular practices and institutions.

4 Two Concepts of Pluralism

Following a suggestion of Raymond Geuss, it can be argued that an important contrast be drawn between two competing conceptions of pluralism. According to Geuss, there is a moderate view of pluralism that is either supportive of, or, at the least, is compatible with most forms of liberalism. The other version is more 'existentialist' in character. We can call this a form of 'deep pluralism'. Here, the dilemmas of radical choice, decision and sacrifice between competing and conflicting values are regarded as being of central significance. This more existentialist version of the response to pluralism is much less sanguine about its possible coherence with liberalism. It also tends towards a tragic vision of history and politics. Similarly, Steven Lukes has noted the presence of two powerful images at work in discussions of pluralism. Surveying the debates about pluralism and the problem of incommensurability, he has pointed to the contrast between the use of metaphors of 'trade-off' and those of 'sacrifice'. Clearly, there is a large gulf between those who prefer to see the problem in terms of one or other of these metaphors. The fact that one is derived from the world of economic exchange and the other from that of religious belief confirms the difference of understanding here.[38]

Geuss illustrates the difference between these two versions of pluralism in the following way. He argues that, according to the liberal version:

> there is a plurality of goods among which one must choose without there being any clear criterion for judging one good to be uniquely the best. The tacit image of the world presupposed by the liberal version is of a place full of goodies with plenty for everyone: let all enter into the banquet of life and take their pick. There are limits to how much any one person can eat, and so eating some things carries a cost, the cost of not being able to eat other things that might in principle be equally tasty. The existentialist version is less sanguine: it is not just the case that one must choose, but choosing one good carries with it a cost that goes beyond the mere opportunity cost of missing out on other goods; this cost may, and usually will, include inflicting pain or visiting evil on oneself, or on others. The existentialist table is a small one; the crowd around it large.[39]

Geuss suggests that we ought to think of 'the conceptual framework of contemporary politics' as a 'highly complex abstract object' for which both versions of pluralism are relevant. Following on from this, the general tendency to focus attention upon the liberal account ought not to be at the expense of recognition of the more existentialist version. It is for this reason that Max Weber's ideas become significant because, in many ways, they exemplify this more tragic and pessimistic vision of politics. Despite the tension between these two views in his work, there is, ultimately, an emphasis upon the resigned recognition of the importance and value of the persistence of conflict and disagreement in politics. What stands out in Weber's work is the importance he placed upon the more 'existentialist' version of the problem of pluralism, which is allied with an awareness of the inevitably tragic dimension in political life. The contemporary significance of this resides in the fact that the recent recognition of pluralism constituting a political problem has, despite the conceptual refinement introduced by a more analytical philosophical approach, not advanced very far in its response to the problem as Weber described it. There is some truth in the claim that one reason for this is due to a large part of the debate taking place within a conceptual framework that has a strong tendency to abstract the existence of value pluralism from a more explicitly and conventionally understood political context of the centrality of power, rule and conflict. More troubling too, perhaps, is the suspicion that no compelling answer acceptable to all is currently available or ever likely to be available.

A similar argument has been put forward by Gerald Gaus. He distinguishes between 'radical' and 'reasonable' versions of the idea of pluralism. Both versions accept the general thesis of the existence of plural and conflicting values. The radical pluralist, however, argues that there can be no single rational ranking of social and political values. Ultimately, the situation is one of a pure choice between conflicting values – a choice not directed by reason alone. The less radical 'reasonable' view allows that 'our powers of reasoning are inconclusive on many complex matters of science, morality, and politics', but not that these matters are necessarily indeterminate.[40]

Gaus also, in a way that resembles Weber's theme of 'disenchantment', places the debate about pluralism within the context of a modern age of 'post-Enlightenment'. This is taken to mean that political theorizing in the modern world takes place within a radically new intellectual environment. This poses a particularly difficult problem for political thought in general and for liberal thought in particular. Most liberal political thinkers have been particularly influenced by the dominant Enlightenment idea that a convergence of moral and political ideas would be the natural outcome of the free exercise of human reason. At the same time, they have also been troubled by the opposing idea that the natural outcome of the free use of reason might not necessarily lead to a convergence of political beliefs and opinion.

The result is that, on the one hand, we have a generally pessimistic vision of 'polytheistic pluralism' that is represented in a strong form in the work of Max Weber, who describes it as 'the war of the gods'. On the other hand, there is an array of more optimistic contemporary political thinkers, represented in particular by John Rawls, who have responded to this problem. In general terms, their answer has largely been to accept the hypothesis of a 'war of the gods' and the reality of a pluralist universe of values, but, in one way or another, to avoid the more pessimistic conclusions drawn by Weber and other like-minded political thinkers. Put simply, the issue seems to break down to one straightforward question: given 'the fact of pluralism' are there any general principles to which we can all agree? Or, as Gaus puts it, 'is an ordered politics based on mutual respect, and aiming at justice, still possible in the modern world of deep reasonable disagreement about values and the ends of life?'[41] If there are such principles, the question remains concerning their scope and depth. If genuine and significant agreement on matters of political substance is our aim, the message delivered by Weber is, generally, a pessimistic one. Although the possibility of agreement cannot be denied, the reality of deep and persistent disagreement regarding moral and political questions certainly cannot be ignored either. Most contemporary political thinkers, and especially those generally thought of as within the liberal camp, have spent a large amount of energy arguing for some grounding for general principles as a counterweight to the demands of pluralism. For example, one of the most influential responses to this problem, the political liberalism of John Rawls, has attempted to redefine the problem away from attachment to a metaphysical thesis about the nature of value, and has focussed upon the problem of reasonable disagreement which, it is argued, can be separated from more controversial philosophical ideas about the nature of value pluralism.

But why think of the lack of agreement as being necessarily a bad thing? There seems to be a deep assumption, encouraged by some forms of contemporary liberalism, that a sufficient degree of agreement is implicit within the culture of most modern western societies, or even among all human societies. If this is absent, it does not follow that it is something we ought to aim for. But why not argue the reverse? Why assume, as so many seem to, that 'a state of conflict' is 'the sign of a vice, or a defect, or a malfunctioning. It is not a deviation from the normal state of a city or of a nation, and it is not a deviation from the normal course of a person's experience.'[42] There is a long tradition of political thinking that sees disagreement, conflict and disharmony as central and unavoidable characteristics of the political condition. The debate about pluralism in modern political thought is, to a large degree, not so much a concern with the philosophical problem of the nature and source of value, important as that is, but with the problem of coping with the persistence of disagreement. This leads, in turn, to the question of how we are to understand the meaning of political disagreement and how we are to cope with it. Nevertheless, whether or not political theory can or ought to avoid the kind of metaphysical commitments involved in making judgements about these questions is a controversial and open question.

It can be argued that one of the advantages of the debates about pluralism is that they have exposed some of the weaknesses and inadequacies that have characterized the intellectual style of much contemporary political theory. For instance, it is clear that reflection upon the nature of pluralism and disagreement has demonstrated the inadequacy of the idea that political philosophy can be essentially nothing other than a form of applied moral philosophy. This may be an appropriate model in many cases. The danger, however, is that if it is taken to apply to the whole domain of political life, then there is a strong temptation to avoid a confrontation with those topics and problems that fall outside the normal concerns of applied ethics. For example, although the construction of 'ideal theory' clearly has its uses and one could argue that it has been a feature of political thought since Plato, it would be a great mistake to restrict the political imagination to the intricacies of abstraction and idealization that this kind of theorizing seems to require. It is in this sense that we ought to be on guard against the constant tendency among academic political theorists to ignore the 'inconvenient facts' expressed in what Bernard Williams has called 'platitudes about politics'.[43] One of these inconvenient facts is the propensity to forget that those we disagree with politically are often also our opponents or, even, our enemies, and cannot realistically be thought of as if they are no more than fellow participants in a seminar. Furthermore, it is a mistake to consider we are justified in thinking that our political opponent is always bound to be morally wrong. The debate about value pluralism among political theorists, it can be argued, ought to direct our attention towards a consideration of the autonomy of the political domain and to make us more on guard against the seductive appeal of the various forms of reductionism always on offer. It is here that some of the concerns raised by critics of Anglo-American theory (sometimes influenced by a mixture of ideas drawn from postmodernism and Carl Schmitt) have some relevance. The question here is whether the correct understanding of the nature of pluralism reveals the unavoidable contingency, arbitrariness and immunity from moral claims as the true reality of 'the political'.[44]

Is not necessary to seek an uncritical source of inspiration in the work of Carl Schmitt in order to gain some understanding of the peculiarity, along with the central role, that politics plays as an activity, or range of activities, among other human practices. The relationship between politics and moral or value pluralism is complicated. What has to be recognized in making sense of our idea of 'the political' is that 'the domain of political positions is controversial in a primordial sense in which the domain of moral demands and appraisals is not'.[45] Aurel Kolnai is one of the few philosophers or political thinkers who explicitly discussed this question. He pointed out that a difficulty arises here because opposing political positions often seem to imply opposing moral attitudes 'essentially, yet in a peculiar, limited and ambiguous fashion'. It would be a mistake, however, to think that moral agreement necessarily guarantees political agreement. In fact, general moral agreement can just as easily contribute to the existence of deep disagreement over particular political questions. In the same manner opposed political positions, call them left and right, might both appeal to the same moral code but differ over their interpretation and application in particular circumstances. In other words, there is a high degree of underdetermination, and neither the moral nor the political side of the equation ought to be taken as foundational. In fact, it is not difficult to imagine situations where political disagreement is intensified precisely because there is an underlying moral agreement. Following this line of thought, and to repeat a commonplace observation, disagreement, conflict and division are constitutive elements of politics. The existence of value pluralism, understood either as an aspect of modernity or as a perennial feature of human association, must then be seen as contributing to the depth and complexity of political existence. It says something about the current state of political philosophy that such a thought that will strike many as blindingly obvious has to be restated. This ought not to come as too much of a surprise. To paraphrase Bernard Williams, the work of political philosophers very often consists of reminding other political philosophers of truths about human society that are very well known to most adult human beings who are not themselves political philosophers.[46]

Although there is a high degree of continuity in the various discussions of pluralism in modern political thought, it becomes clear on close inspection that the concept of pluralism has been used in different ways and with different purposes in mind. It is not at all self-evident, for instance, that Isaiah Berlin and John Rawls share the same concerns or see the relevance of the problem in the same way when they are talking about pluralism. Perhaps it makes more sense to think of the meaning of the concept of pluralism in terms of its use in particular intellectual and political contexts. Pluralism can itself be regarded as a contestable concept. While avoiding the question of whether it is an 'essentially' contestable concept, and departing a little from its original usage by Gallie, it is important to recognize the inevitability of disagreement about the meaning and implications of pluralism itself.[47] If the thesis of value pluralism is right, in either its epistemic or metaphysical versions, then we ought not to be surprised to encounter a pluralism about pluralism. This is not to deny a continuity of concerns running from, for example, Weber to Rawls and Habermas. Nevertheless, political theorists have interpreted and defined the concept of pluralism in terms of their own central intellectual and political concerns. The importance given to the problem of pluralism by political thinkers derives its sense from its contribution to the wider questions that give direction to their work. This is one reason for approaching the topic primarily in terms of the way it has presented itself as a problem or topic in the work of some of the most interesting modern political thinkers, rather than as a set of disembodied concepts and problems.[48] A clear example of this is provided by the way in which Isaiah Berlin's account of the nature and value of pluralism was formulated in, and takes on its distinct character from, the context of his understanding of the nature of totalitarianism and the clash of ideologies in the Cold War. This is not to claim that this is the only context in terms of which his concern with the problem of value pluralism can be understood. But it does illuminate much about the work that he required the concept to do.

Critics of that modern version of academic liberalism, represented in the work of political thinkers such as Rawls, Walzer and Habermas, have pointed out that one of the striking peculiarities of their work is that they want to bring together under one theoretical roof both a recognition of pluralism with regard to concepts of the good and the broadest possible consensus with regard to concepts of the right. Liberal theorists, it is argued, typically claim that 'living securely with deep and widespread disagreements about the best way to live requires a broad, if not very deep, agreement on liberal principles of justice'. The one basic and potentially destructive problem for this argument appears obvious. It is that 'our disagreements about justice are often just as deep and intractable as our disagreements about the best way to live'.[49] The result is that contemporary theorists who want to argue for the compatibility of their own prescription for justice with the pluralism that they clearly recognize have typically been forced to argue that beneath the apparent facts of pluralism and disagreement there must be some agreement about basic principles. We ought not to be too surprised to find how frequently it is claimed that the required consensus has, in fact, been discovered. The problem, however, is that it has been found in too many different places. These locations are, for example, 'implicit in relatively uncontroversial norms of rationality; hidden among the assumptions that make effective communication possible; embedded in our shared democratic public culture; or rooted in the historical meanings of different social goods'.[50] The problem here is, of course, that these proposals are no less controversial than the competing conceptions of the good that they are meant to neutralize. The distinctiveness of much liberal theory, it can be argued, is not to be found simply in its concern with pluralism but, rather, in its attempt to neutralize it by appealing, for instance, to the way in which an implicit consensus can be made explicit. Several versions of this thesis can be identified. Apart from the claim that some form of consensus does actually exist, even if implicitly, within all societies, the significant contention being put forward is that we are obliged to reach consensus and that it would be a good thing to do so.[51] The argument here, on the other hand, is that there is no need to regard either pluralism or disagreement as pathological and in need of complete repair. If pluralism and disagreement are unavoidable components of the subject matter of politics, then we ought to avoid blaming political theorists if they take them so seriously that they become deeply sceptical of all attempts to overcome or neutralize them.[52]

5 An Outline of the Argument

When discussing the problems raised by value pluralism for political theory it is natural to admit to some uncertainty about the best way to proceed. I have chosen to concentrate my attention mainly upon those modern political thinkers I consider to best exemplify the compexity, tensions and dilemmas that are the inevitable outcome of reflection upon this topic. Of course, approaching the issue in a seemingly more analytical and problem- rather than author-focused manner has its advantages. However, in political theory, this is more likely than not to produce a rather dry discussion that is thought to be more professionally respectable. The fact that such approaches are more easily packaged for presentation to funding bodies with appeals for their 'relevance' for imagined policy proposals is also a factor not to be dismissed. On inspection, such accounts, despite their claims to some form of superior analytical bite, usually end up discussing the arguments of a select group of favoured theorists. More fundamentally, this style of inquiry rests upon a particular, but equally controversial, view of the nature and purpose of political philosophy. This is to see political philosophy as a problem-solving activity that, in reality, mimics a particular idea of how the natural sciences are presumed to operate. Alternatively, political philosophy can be understood as an activity in which we attach more importance to the asking of questions than we do to the answers provided.[53] If we accept this is a reasonable way of progressing, then it seems obvious that we have much to learn from looking at the way in which some of the most acute political thinkers of the twentieth century have tried to make sense of the problem of value pluralism.

I have concentrated my attention upon a group of political thinkers who have directly taken up the challenge of value pluralism and made it a central feature of their work. There are, of course, others who could be included, but given the limitations of space and energy it makes sense to focus upon a relatively small number of significant theorists. In addition, and in support of their selection, there are clear and direct lines of influence between them.

Chapter 2 discusses the work of a group of political theorists who draw, in different degrees, pessimistic conclusions from their reflections upon pluralism. They are pessimistic in the sense that they see value pluralism as setting limitations upon the practice of politics and political philosophy. The first major thinker to be considered is Max Weber. Why start with Weber? One reason is that even if not everyone would agree that he was the 'most important political philosopher of the twentieth century', the power of his insight into the major problems that have come to define modern politics is undeniable.[54] Weber thought longer and harder than most about the relationship between moral dilemmas and the reality of politics. Weber's images of 'disenchantment' and 'polytheism' have had a persistent influence upon modern political theory. This is not always recognized.

While Isaiah Berlin has not acknowledged any direct influence from Weber in the formulation of his version of value pluralism, he has admitted their affinity of ideas. Berlin is generally credited with the introduction of the idea of value pluralism into Anglo-American political philosophy. Although it is possible to point to various precursors, this is undeniably true. Nevertheless, the central idea of the pluralism of values in Berlin's essays was not the main focus of interest in the early reception of his work. It took some time for the message to sink in. Although some of Berlin's critics have compared him unfavourably with Weber, pointing, for example, to the absence of a sense of drama and tragedy in his work, it is undeniable that the rediscovery of the topic of value pluralism owes more to his work than it does to that of any other political thinker.

Berlin's account of value pluralism has not been without its critics. John Gray's work stands out as a sympathetic but critical exploration of what many see as a central tension in Berlin's work. Gray's distinctive version of 'agonistic liberalism' and of a politics of 'modus vivendi' is a controversial development of what he understands to be the true implications of Berlin's pluralism.

The account of value pluralism developed by Weber, Berlin and Gray is marked, despite the important differences of emphasis between them, by a general air of pessimism. This is a pessimism concerning the nature and limits of both politics and political philosophy. The pessimistic conclusions that can be drawn from contemplation of the implications of pluralism for politics are shown in the work of Stuart Hampshire. He insists that his own argument 'against monotheism' is far stronger than that offered by Berlin's account of value pluralism. Hampshire's slogan that 'all determination is negation' reveals the metaphysical underpinnings of his 'philosophy of conflict'.[55] Inspired by Spinoza, Hampshire presents a picture of unavoidable conflicts of interest and of conceptions of the good. Our powers of rational argument provide a weak protection against the 'unchanging horrors of human life'.

The political philosophies of John Rawls and Jürgen Habermas, discussed in chapter 3, share a concern with the problem of value pluralism. Rawls was clearly influenced by the work of both Berlin and Weber. The construction of a viable alternative to the more pessimistic implications of their work is a central theme in his political philosophy. Habermas, with his background in the philosophy and social theory of the Frankfurt School, can be understood, to a large degree, as being guided by an extended dialogue with the ghost of Max Weber. When Rawls and Habermas engaged in direct debate with each other the centrality of the questions that Weber had first raised became evident. Although there are some hints of despair in Rawls's political philosophy, it is true to say that both he and Habermas converge upon a more optimistic understanding of the perils of pluralism. Reasonable citizens, even if living in a disenchanted world, can learn to cope with value pluralism.

The deeper significance of the arguments over value pluralism concerns the fact that they lead to consideration of a series of deep disagreements about the nature of politics and of political theory. The view that favours the search for stability, agreement and reconciliation has been challenged by a growing recognition of the permanence of pluralism, with endemic disagreement understood as an unavoidable component of the human political condition.[56]

2

Pluralism and Pessimism

In an interesting and revealing footnote, John Rawls quotes Isaiah Berlin's argument that 'there is no social world without loss'. In this footnote, Rawls compares the views of Isaiah Berlin and Max Weber on the problem of pluralism. He notes that a view similar to Berlin's is often attributed to Weber, but this, he argues, is a mistake. There is a marked difference between them. Berlin, according to Rawls, sees the world of value as fully objective. No actual social world can accommodate the full range of values. Values are incompatible with one another and impose conflicting requirements upon individuals and institutions. Hence 'the fact that there is no social world without loss is itself a consequence of the nature of values and the world'. On the other hand, Max Weber, according to Rawls, has a view of values that is voluntaristic and sceptical. According to this interpretation, Weber was devoted to a vision where 'the conflict of subjective commitments and resolute wills' is a major source of political tragedy.[1]

The correctness of Rawls's interpretation of Weber is debatable. Although this reference to Weber disappeared in the equivalent section of 'Political Liberalism', it reappeared, with minor modification, in the later restatement of his theory of justice.[2] This suggests that Rawls remained convinced of the significance of the ideas of both Berlin and Weber for his own formulation of the problem of pluralism. Despite the obvious differences between them, Weber, Berlin and Rawls are three of the most important theorists who have responded to the political implications of value pluralism. It is possible, however, to see a progressive movement in Berlin's and Rawls's political thought away from Weber's apprehension over what he regarded as the pessimistic, tragic and dramatic consequences of the experience of value pluralism under modern conditions. Nevertheless, these aspects of value pluralism never disappear completely. It is striking, for example, that Rawls admits in this same footnote and elsewhere that the tragic features that worried both Berlin and Weber cannot be completely eradicated from his own vision of the 'realistic utopia' of a just liberal society.

1 Weber's Values

Rawls is right to point out that there are clear differences of concern and emphasis in the ways that the idea of pluralism has been understood, as well as in the place that it occupies in the concerns of different political thinkers. It would be a mistake to assume, when political thinkers such as Berlin, Weber and Rawls talk about pluralism, that they necessarily have exactly the same problems in mind or that they are moved by the same set of concerns. The absence of an overlapping consensus between them does not rule out the fact that they do share some important ideas. Nevertheless, it would be an error to overlook the clear differences between political thinkers such as Max Weber, who worked in the shadow of both Kant and Nietzsche, and the later contributions of thinkers such as Isaiah Berlin and John Rawls who despite the breadth of their intellectual concerns were firmly rooted in the modern Anglo-American tradition of moral and political philosophy.

One essential difference here is that Weber's political pessimism seemed to lead him into an impasse. Weber shared with many other German political thinkers and philosophers of his time a fear that Europe was entering an age of general cultural and moral decline. Weber and many of his contemporaries were concerned to a large degree with a particular vision of the fate of the west. A central component of this image was exemplified by the victory of instrumental rationality over the claims

of reason. This cultural predicament was, in turn, accentuated
by the increasingly unfettered operation of the will to power.

The intellectual situation is entirely different with Berlin
and Rawls. Both were working from within an established
liberal and democratic tradition. They both regarded pluralism
as a problem both of and for liberalism, but not necessarily as
a fatal threat to it. However, there is another difference of
emphasis between the three theorists. Berlin and Weber,
despite the differences between them, were generally not as
optimistic as Rawls seemed to be about the implications of
pluralism. They were not overly sanguine about the future
prospects for liberal regimes. Furthermore, they possessed a
strong sense of the way in which the claims made by political
philosophers are shaped and limited, in varying degrees, by
historical circumstances. In contrast, a striking fact about the
work of some more recent contributors to this debate, such as
Rawls and Habermas, is that despite their recognition of the
difficulties they are, on balance, far more optimistic about our
ability to cope with the problem of pluralism and of preserving
and strengthening the institutions of the liberal constitutional
state.

It is probably not too much of an exaggeration to say that
much modern western political thought is haunted by the
ghost of Max Weber. This is not to claim that there is a widespread recognition of the significance of Weber's ideas. However,
a great deal of modern political thought can be read as if it is
responding to Weber's central arguments about the nature of
politics in the modern western state. In particular, his ideas of
value pluralism, described in terms of a permanent 'war of the
gods', and of 'the disenchantment of the world' seem to have
had a remarkably long life. Considering Weber's own views
about the relatively short natural life expectancy that social
and political concepts ought to expect, he would probably find
this quite surprising. Although the origin and persistence of
pervasive ideas of disenchantment and value pluralism are not
always openly acknowledged, these ideas can often be found
in the implicit background of much of the thinking about the
problem of pluralism.

Interpretations of Weber's political thought are bound to be
controversial. However, it can be argued that Max Weber raised
a series of questions that provide the basis for a powerful criti-

cism of the philosophical ideas underlying much of modern political and social theorizing. It is still a plausible option to argue that, generally speaking, attempts made by contemporary political theorists to respond to the challenge put forward by Weber have failed to be entirely convincing. This seems to suggest a troubling impasse in modern political thought. Modern political theory has increasingly come to accept a version of the Weberian vision of value pluralism as a genuine problem. At the same time, it can be argued, we are also – often without being aware of it – held captive by Weber's images and metaphors of 'disenchantment', 'the iron cage' ('the steel casing' is more accurate) and the 'war of the gods'. Although it can be argued that there is no necessary connection between value pluralism and disenchantment, it is also true that as far as Weber was concerned there is, at least, a strong affinity between these two forces in the modern world. The deeper the disenchantment, the more intense the struggle between values is likely to be. It is not necessary to claim that all or most modern political thinkers necessarily have had Weber in mind when thinking about pluralism. Nevertheless, it seems undeniable that Weberian motifs and themes have shaped, to a large degree, much of the framework of modern political and social thought. In fact, even when unaware of it, modern political thinkers are often, in effect, responding to or repeating Weber's questions.

Weber offers the clearest and most challenging version of an 'existentialist' or tragic version of pluralism. Although the sources of Weber's pessimistic vision of the political condition of modern mankind can be placed within a specifically German tradition of political and philosophical thought, its significance transcends its own time and place of origin. This, however, is not to say that the news is all bad. Although the dominant motif in Weber's pluralistic vision is pessimistic, later thinkers have sought to temper it and in doing so have reinterpreted the problem and meaning of pluralism in the light of changing intellectual and political concerns. If John Rawls's argument that the aims of political philosophy depend upon the society it addresses is correct, then we ought to expect that the significance attributed to the problem of pluralism will acquire different nuances of meaning in different times and in different places.

The first point that has to be made is that, although Weber did not use the terms 'pluralism' or 'value pluralism', the ideas implied by these terms are clearly of fundamental importance for his political thought. His central claim is that we live in a world characterized by the existence of 'unbridgeably divergent ultimate evaluations'.[3] In a famous passage, Weber argues that:

> the different value systems of the world stand in conflict with one another. The elder Mill, whose philosophy I would not otherwise wish to praise but who was right on this point, said in his old age: if one proceeds from pure experience, one arrives at polytheism. That is superficially formulated and sounds para-doxical, but there is truth in it . . . different gods struggle with each other and will do for all time. It is just like in the ancient world, which was not yet disenchanted with its gods and demons, but in another sense. Just as Hellenic man sacrificed on this occasion to Aphrodite and on another to Apollo, and above all as everybody sacrificed to the gods of his city-things are still the same today, but disenchanted and divested of the mythical but inwardly genuine flexibility of those customs.[4]

It is important to note that, contrary to what is often asserted, Weber's argument does not deny the possibility of and, indeed, the need for rational debate about the nature of values and their implications. Nor does his understanding of value rule out the possibility of a 'normative ethics'. The difficult question, however, is whether or not there is an avoidable residue of irrationalism at the core of his view of the clash of values. Weber made it clear that, as far as he was concerned, it is only through the rational examination of the meaning and implica-tions of our basic ideas and values that we could hope to achieve the clarity that he considered necessary for living as an autonomous and responsible citizen in a modern democratic and disenchanted world. However, Weber was quite clear that the rational discussion of values can itself be a contributory factor in our awareness and understanding of the potential and real depth of political disagreement. Of course, Weber goes even further in his insistence on the centrality of struggle and conflict in political life. He argues that any evaluation of another set of values is always made from the standpoint of one's own values. Furthermore, this act of evaluation and criti-cism cannot be anything other than a struggle between those ideals and one's own.[5] It is not surprising that Weber was deeply sceptical of the claim that the results of philosophical or sociological inquiries into the nature of our moral and political values could provide solutions for practical problems. Such inquiry could never completely transcend the deep disagreements that are likely to arise from the existence of plural and conflicting values. This is especially true for political questions. Clearly, there is a deep presumption of the existence and persistence of pervasive and recalcitrant disagreement in his understanding of the implications of value pluralism for the political world.

In considering the idea of justice, for example, Weber argues that it can be regarded, in modern terminology, as an 'essentially contested concept'. There is no procedure or technique that can deliver an unambiguous and non-controversial decision in favour of one or other of the conflicting interpretations of this internally complex concept. It would be a dogmatic error to claim that there is or can only be one correct interpretation. Political disagreement of this kind can be regarded as a form of 'faultless disagreement'.[6] If we take his example of the revolutionary syndicalist and the pacifist discussing the merits of their respective moral and political commitments, each can strive to understand the other and to clarify the logic of their arguments.[7] However, there is no reason to assume that they will or ought to finally end up agreeing with each other. Weber makes it clear that, in his view, there is no non-controversial procedure that can provide a definitive decision between competing concepts of justice. According to his account, we can and, indeed, do have a duty to analyse political standpoints and to represent them in their most coherent form, but when it comes to the ultimate commitments upon which they are based – their metaphysical premises – then he argues that these can never be demonstrated to the satisfaction of all relevant parties. This is not to deny that political standpoints are immune from criticism. There is nothing in this argument that says, for example, that a political standpoint cannot be shown to be vulnerable on the grounds of its mistaken understanding of a scientific fact or theory, or on the grounds of faulty logic and a badly constructed argument. The basic point is that Weber was deeply sceptical of the idea that either philosophy or social science could provide a neutral standpoint in terms of which the demands of conflicting values could be adjudicated. In Weber's account, value pluralism is taken to be both a fact and a theory. The recognition of the sheer fact of the existence of a plurality of values is supported by a theory about the nature of those values. Of course, the idea that there is, in fact, a world of plural values is itself a highly theoretical interpretation.

In order to obtain a clear picture of Weber's idea of the problem of value pluralism, it is necessary to discount most of the conventional wisdom that has permeated, until relatively recently, most accounts of his thought. When looked at with 'fresh eyes', as Wilhelm Hennis has urged, we see that Weber's discussion of what we would now call value pluralism is more complex and challenging than has often been recognized.

It is clear that Weber's idea of pluralism runs deep. Value pluralism and the conflict of values occupy the centre of his diagnosis of the culture of modernity. In a forceful statement, Weber asserts that:

> the fate of an epoch that has eaten of the tree of knowledge is that it must know that we cannot learn the meaning of the world from the results of its analysis, be it ever so perfect; it must rather be in a position to create this meaning itself. It must recognize that general views of life and the universe can never be the products of increasing empirical knowledge, and that the highest ideals, which move us most forcefully, are always formed only in the struggle with other ideals which are just as sacred to others as ours are to us.[8]

The pluralism of values includes an irresolvable conflict between both our first-order values and between our second-order theories of value. The idea of an 'ethic of responsibility' plays a central role in his exposition of the problem. The 'crucial point' for Weber is that there are two 'fundamentally different, irreconcilably opposed maxims': the 'ethic of principled conviction' and the 'ethic of responsibility'.[9] These ethical theories and the maxims derived from them are in a state of perpetual conflict that cannot itself be resolved by ethical means alone. There is no higher ethic or principle that can be appealed to without encountering the charge of circularity.

Throughout his work, Weber stressed the unavoidable nature of conflicts between irreconcilable values and ethical standpoints. Of course, he recognized that most of the time the majority of us go through life without worrying too much that our world is constituted to a large degree by overlapping, inter-penetrating and often conflicting realms of value. He also rec-ognized that very few people possess a unified and totally consistent body of beliefs and ideas. However, there are times when we are sharply reminded of the fact that our lives are bound up in 'irreconcilably antagonistic values'. In saying this, Weber was pointing out that the difficulty involved in the case of plural and conflicting values does not simply reside in the intuitively familiar case of what Bernard Williams refers to as 'two-party conflict', but with the more intractable case of 'one-person conflict'.[10] The conflict of values exists both between and within persons. Weber recognized and stressed a point often made by modern moral philosophers, to the effect that much inquiry concerned with problems of objectivity has con-centrated on two-party conflict: 'where the problem is that of resolving disagreement: it is generally assumed that the parties have each their harmonious set of value-beliefs. Accompanying that, usually, is an assumption that, whatever may turn out to be the case with two-party conflicts, at any rate one-person conflict must be capable of being rationally resolved.'[11]

Weber's account of the conflict of values can be described as being moderately existentialist. There is a constant emphasis upon the necessity for the individual to be aware of the need, whenever it arises, to make decisions, 'ultimate decisions', between 'God' and the 'Devil'. Weber refers to Plato, as he often does at crucial junctures in his work, when he speaks of living a life that rises above 'our routine daily existence', when we have to choose our own fate, in order to become aware of the meaning of our life. It can reasonably be inferred from the text that Weber has Plato's powerful image of the cave in mind. However, the difference between Plato and Weber (and most other modern political thinkers) is that, as far as politics is concerned, it seems clear to him that we ought not to expect the appearance of philosopher rulers (kings) to show us the way out of the cave.[12] Although it is sometimes argued that there is something 'Platonic' in Weber's talk of intellectual aristocracies or of charismatic political leaders, this cannot be quite right. This kind of interpretation runs aground on Weber's own understanding of the nature of philosophy. As far as

Weber was concerned, in the wake of what he and many others understood as Nietzsche's devastating criticism of the European intellectual tradition, the age in which philosophers could legislate the truth, and, in particular, the political truth, was long gone. There is no Archimedean point outside the war of the gods. Political theory can never completely transcend the world of politics where the pluralism of values is often experienced in its most intense form. Political philosophy cannot escape the recognition of its historicity and its own political character. The political philosopher can never step completely outside the cave.

Nevertheless, Weber allows that when it comes to the problem of the relationship between means and ends, as well as the conflict between incommensurable values, there is the possibility of compromise as well as of radical choice. Weber's basic point is that in our practice of choice or of compromise we cannot, or ought not, to rely upon the support of any kind of decision procedure that the sciences, natural or human, or philosophy might claim to offer. However, although it is true that Weber does speak of the possibility of compromise in moral and political disagreement, the overwhelming impression that he gives is that compromise will always occur within a broader context in which, when it comes to the 'war of the gods', there is ultimately no escape from the necessity of making choices, often tragic, where the prevailing image will be of sacrifice rather than of trade-offs.[13]

It is a fundamental misunderstanding of Weber's intentions to argue, as does Hilary Putnam, that Weber is to blame for reintroducing a simple version of the fact–value distinction into modern political and social thought. This popular charge is based on the idea that it is impossible to establish the truth of a value judgement that would be acceptable to all relevant rational persons.[14] Weber's argument, according to Putnam, is 'a disguised form' of majoritarianism. Putnam interprets Weber as resting his claims concerning the fact–value distinction on the belief that we can 'get the agreement of educated people on "positive science" whereas we cannot get such an agreement on ethical values'.[15] In fact, Weber is quite clear that his argument has nothing to do with the number of persons who might or might not agree to an ethical argument. He points out that there are many available examples where we can see more agreement about, for instance, a description of someone as being 'dishonest' than we might find among natural scientists concerning the interpretation of a scientific fact.[16]

There is a strong conceptual connection between the account of the conflict of values and the central role of concepts of conflict and power in Weber's political thought. This reinforces his understanding of the autonomous nature of the realm of moral and political value. Consequently, Weber, in a way that is echoed in much recent moral and political theory, is pointing to the nature of conflicts of value in a non-reductionist way and, hence, to the autonomy of the political.[17] Value conflicts have a specific character and ought not to be regarded as straightforward reflections of something else, such as conflicts of class or of national interests.

The account of the 'polytheism of values' offered by Weber is bound up with his vision of 'disenchantment'. Although there is no necessary connection between value pluralism and disenchantment, the two ideas have a clear 'elective affinity' in Weber's thought. At the heart of Weber's conception of pluralism and disenchantment, there lies the (often concealed) influence of Nietzsche. It is probably this influence that more than anything else separates Weber's pluralism from that of later liberal theorists such as Berlin and Rawls.

> Weber accepted without reservation Nietzsche's diagnosis of the time: God is dead. He treated it as the 'basic fact' that we are fated to live in a 'godless time, without prophets'. All objective order of values deriving from the Christian conception of God breaks down. Weber is the first to have drawn the most radical scientific conclusions from Nietzsche's diagnosis of nihilism. It is the fate of our epoch to have eaten of the tree of knowledge: that is, with Nietzsche to have turned the consistency of the Christian pathos of truth, of intellectual honesty, itself against all hitherto-prevailing values.[18]

In the Nietzschean interpretation, it is the death of God that sets the modern world apart. It is at one and the same time a catastrophe and a challenge. For Nietzsche, the 'greatest recent event – that "God is dead", that the belief in the Christian god has become unbelievable – is already beginning to cast its first shadows over Europe'.[19]

This is the most important intellectual context for Weber's account of value pluralism. By accepting the Nietszchean interpretation, we live in age that has witnessed both the death of the traditional absolutes and our faith in the possibility of such absolutes. Under the shadow of western nihilism, the highest values devalue themselves. The political implications are immense. All claims made by political faiths and ideologies are susceptible to sceptical self-destruction. Leo Strauss's interpretation of Nietzsche is a dramatic way of understanding this transformation. He sees Nietzsche as being responsible for 'the third wave of modernity' that introduced a deep historical consciousness into European thought. This, in turn, is marked by a tragic and pessimistic vision of the essential insolubility of fundamental political problems, such as the 'politico-theological problem', and the absence of any meaning for ideas of progress or of a final reconciliation in history.[20] This analysis of modernity also points to a crisis in political philosophy. One implication of this interpretation is the thesis that the classical tradition of political thought, from Plato to Marx, has come to an end.[21] This was the conclusion reached by Weber, Arendt and other, mainly German, political thinkers influenced by the Nietzschean intellectual revolution. If this interpretation is correct, it implies a radical rethinking of the role of the political philosopher working under the conditions of a pluralistic modernity.

Weber, it is clear, accepted Nietzsche's diagnosis of his age. He accepted that it is a basic and unavoidable fact about the modern world that God is dead. Weber was the first major thinker to recognize the political implications of this idea. The world in which we live is one that is subject to a radical disenchantment. Weber, in particular, accepts Nietzsche's account of the origin of Christianity as a universal religion of love, based upon the Sermon on the Mount, that stands in radical opposition to other moral orders. Weber and Nietzsche both reject this ethic. For them, human life is an endless struggle between man and man. There is no objective order of values that we can appeal to in this struggle. The role of the 'cultural sciences' or the 'sciences of reality', as he called them, is to attempt to understand and come to terms with the present situation and its genealogy. Weber also adheres to Nietzsche's 'perspectivism'. All scholarship is undertaken from a particular value-laden standpoint and there is no possibility of achieving any kind of synthesis of all possible standpoints.

For Weber, one important source of meaning is to be found in the struggle between the many new and old gods who have emerged from their graves. It is in the clash of ultimate stand-points, above all else, that the individual can be forced to 'give an account of the ultimate meaning of his own actions'.[22] As far as Weber was concerned, the 'highest ideals' are always formed in the struggle with different ideals which are as sacred to others as ours are to us.[23] The struggle of ideas and the conflict of values form the essential context within which it is possible for us to understand what our own values really are.

Perhaps we can argue that Weber's own disenchantment did not go far enough. Under the influence of Nietzsche (as well as Machiavelli), there is an almost metaphysical belief in the creative power of political struggle. Weber himself sought redemption through commitment to a calling (*Beruf*). There may be some truth in seeing the tension in Weber's thought as deriving from the conflicting demands of being drawn to play simultaneously the roles of a German Socrates and a German Machiavelli.[24] His pluralism was enlisted in the struggle against the illusions of the age, but it is itself tied to a resigned accept-ance of the permanence of relations of power, rule and conflict in human affairs. Above all, it is a counter against all attempts at re-enchantment. The political implication is that there is no necessary connection between the acceptance of pluralism and the support of either liberalism or constitutional democracy. The effect of the central role that value pluralism plays in Weber's political thought is to both draw our attention to the fragility of the institutions of western constitutional states and to defend the space left for individual freedom that they served to protect. Weber's commitment to value pluralism, described in terms of 'the war of the gods', in its stress upon struggle and conflict is intended to have the effect of forcing us to be aware of the meaning and consequences of our decisions and com-mitments. But the centrality of judgement in Weber's account avoids descent into the stark 'decisionism' with which he has often been accused.[25]

2 Isaiah Berlin: Pluralism and the Cosmic Jigsaw Puzzle

In the world of modern Anglo-American political theory, the discovery of the problem of pluralism is generally attributed to the work of Isaiah Berlin. In particular, the publication of his Inaugural Lecture, 'Two Concepts of Liberty', delivered on occupying the Chichele Chair of Political and Social Theory at the University of Oxford in 1958, is taken as the textual origin of the 'pluralist movement' in political theory. This essay was, at first, noticed primarily for the famous distinction between 'positive' and 'negative' liberty that Berlin did so much to popularize. It subsequently became clear that this conceptual distinction itself rested upon the more interesting and controversial thesis of value pluralism.

It is now generally agreed that the idea of the existence of plural and conflicting values is, or has become in the eyes of many contemporary political theorists, the central theme in the political thought of Isaiah Berlin. This is a relatively recent development insofar as Berlin, prior to the emergence of the problem of pluralism as a central topic in political thought, was generally thought of as primarily a historian of political ideas rather than a political philosopher. It might be that Berlin's own self-description, as someone who had abandoned philosophy for the history of ideas, contributed to the general disregard of his account of pluralism by philosophers and political theorists. Charles Taylor has pointed out that Berlin's thesis of pluralism was 'deeply unsettling to the moral theories dominant in his own milieu. It is one of the paradoxes of our intellectual world, which will be increasingly discussed in the future, why this latter point was not realized. The bomb was planted in the academy but somehow failed to go off.'[26] It is also worth noting that these claims made for the significance and originality of Berlin's contribution to political thought have also been challenged, and have encountered considerable scepticism. For example, Ernest Gellner argued forcefully that Berlin's idea of pluralism is both unoriginal and obscure. In particular, Gellner pointed out that Berlin himself refers to some intellectual precursors for this idea of pluralism. Machiavelli, Vico, Herder and Tolstoy are all mentioned in Berlin's essays. However, the problem here is that, in so doing, Berlin seems to undermine his own claims, or, at least, those made on his behalf, for the originality of his idea of pluralism. We can point both to the centrality of tragic conflicts of value in ancient Greek drama and, in more recent times, to such figures (of whom Berlin was clearly more than just aware) as Max Weber and Raymond Aron, for whom the idea of the pluralism of values was a central concern. Clearly, it is of particular interest here to reflect upon Berlin's avoidance of a discussion of Weber's ideas on the problem of plural and conflicting values. As Gellner exclaims, Weber 'didn't merely talk about warring gods, he explored them with unequalled depth. All this is highly relevant, in as far as one of the crucial criticisms which can be made of Berlin's formulation of the rival-gods problem is precisely its sociological thinness, its abstract philosophical formulation.'[27]

Furthermore, for Gellner, the more damaging criticism is that Berlin's pluralism is unable to avoid the charge of relativism. According to Gellner:

> Recognition of conflict as such is nothing new: the novelty lies only in the vigorous affirmation of the finality of the situation. But the affirmation of 'incommensurate values' is relativism, presented in different and more innocuous words. The existence of conflict between values is simply a fact; but incommensurability is a theory, and the theory is relativism.[28]

Nevertheless, Berlin is now generally credited with the achievement of being the modern political thinker who most clearly demonstrated the importance of value pluralism. Others go much further. An example here is Ira Katznelson, who is prepared to ask: 'Why is it so intuitively true that Berlin's work is both correct and bold?'[29] Bernard Williams has pointed out in a more measured tone that Berlin always 'insisted that there exists a plurality of values which conflict with one another, and which are not reducible to one another'. As a consequence, 'we cannot conceive of a situation in which it was true that all value-conflict had been eliminated, and that there had been no loss of value on the way'. Furthermore, it has to be recognized that 'the business of reaffirming and defending the plurality of values is itself a political task'.[30]

Berlin's 'official' view of the nature of political philosophy is informed throughout by the idea that it consists in 'ethics

applied to society' and that, as a consequence, pluralism is now
its central problem. In his essay 'Does Political Theory Still
Exist?' Berlin asks 'the Kantian question': 'In what kind of
world is political philosophy possible?' His answer is that political philosophy is possible 'Only in a world where ends collide'.[31]
Using a term which he himself popularized, Berlin has been
characterized as both an intellectual 'hedgehog' masquerading
as an intellectual 'fox' and as a 'fox' who is really a 'hedgehog'.
This refers to the quotation from the Greek poet Archilocus
that Berlin popularized: 'The fox knows many things, but the
hedgehog knows one big thing.'[32] Whether Berlin is best
described as a hedgehog or a fox, or as neither, it still makes
sense to say that the pluralism of values is his 'big idea'. The
constant reflection upon the meaning and significance of value
pluralism reveals the contents of the 'inner fortress' in Berlin's
political thought.

The task of political philosophy, for Berlin, is to be concerned with the 'examination of the ends of life, human purposes, social and collective. The business of political philosophy
is to examine the validity of various claims made for various
social goals and the justification of the methods of specifying
and attaining these.'[33] What is distinctive about Berlin's
approach to the task of examining the substance of political
ideas and ideals is contained in his stress upon the way in which
moral and political ideas are irreducibly plural. It is clear that
inside the 'inner fortress' in Berlin's political thought there is
a defence of the value of individual liberty allied to the struggle
against totalitarianism. For Berlin, it is clear that the idea of
pluralism is inseparable from his idea of politics. However
attractive an idea this seems to be, it is not thoroughly explored
in his work. Does it mean, for example, that political thinking
would not be possible within a monistic environment?

The fundamental idea of pluralism, which is expressed fairly
consistently throughout his work, rests upon the discovery,
which he tells us he made early in his career, of what he calls
the 'Ionian fallacy'. The basic mistake expressed by this fallacy
is to believe that:

> all genuine questions must have one true answer and one only,
> all the rest being necessarily errors; in the second place, that
> there must be a dependable path towards the discovery of these

truths; in the third place, that the true answers, when found, must necessarily be compatible with one another and form a single whole, for one truth cannot be incompatible with another – this we know a priori. This kind of omniscience was the solution of the cosmic jigsaw puzzle.[34]

Further, Berlin argues that:

> the notion of a perfect whole, the ultimate solution, in which all good things coexist, seems to me to be not merely unattainable – that is a truism – but conceptually incoherent; I do not know what is meant by a harmony of this kind. Some among the Great Goods cannot live together. That is a conceptual truth. We are doomed to choose, and every choice may entail an irreparable loss.[35]

This description of pluralism raises three questions. The first is whether his version of pluralism is clearly distinguishable from relativism. The second question is that of the relationship between liberalism and pluralism. The two questions are connected because, it is argued, if Berlin's pluralism is indistinguishable from relativism, then it follows he cannot show that the liberalism he supports is any more than one political option among many. The third question concerns the role of reason in the choice between incommensurable values.

Berlin's pluralism also asserts the incommensurability of values, but not necessarily their incomparability. These two terms are often confused. Incommensurability is taken to mean that there is no single scale of units of value in terms of which different values or, perhaps, more accurately, different bearers of value could be measured. The term is often used to mean incomparability – the idea, simply, that things, in this case values, cannot be compared. This leads to two controversial questions. Does incommensurability imply incomparability? And if it does, what are the implications for our understanding of practical reason?[36] Berlin's view of pluralism is not always consistent or clear. At times he sees incommensurability as implying incomparability. Further, this leads to an emphasis upon situations of tragic choice in which the agent is put in the position where, for instance, faced with a choice between two equally valued options, he or she cannot act without regret and certainly cannot rely upon any strategy of maximization as, for

example, utilitarians would argue. Nevertheless, insofar as use
of the concept of value implies that evaluation takes place, then
this would lead us to expect that comparison is both possible
and necessary. Confronted with the problem of 'ultimate
values' in the sense of values that are regarded as ends in themselves, Berlin described himself as 'in a sense' an existentialist.
At some point we have no alternative but to say that we are
committed to a certain constellation of values. It is in terms of
these values that we live. In political terms we have to take a
side; we 'plump' for one side rather than the other.[37] This does
not mean that we are barred from analysing the rationality of
values. It would be a mistake to infer that Berlin subscribed to
the view that the concept of rationality could only be applied
to means but not to ends. Some values must be recognized
because they enter into our general understanding of what it
is to be a human being.[38]

Both supporters and critics alike have identified Berlin's
pluralism with relativism. For example Leo Strauss, one of the
early critics, saw Berlin's position as being symptomatic of 'the
crisis of liberalism – of a crisis due to the fact that liberalism
has abandoned its absolutist base and is trying to become
entirely relativistic'.[39] According to Strauss, this account suffers
because it, like so much modern thought, is guilty of abandon-
ing the classical search for the just, the rational, the perfect
society. Looked at from this standpoint, the project of modern
liberalism must fail. In Strauss's view, Berlin's account of pluralism is self-contradictory because political and moral theory
cannot avoid either making or relying upon some distinctions
of an 'absolutist' kind. As an example of this, Strauss points to
Berlin's statement that commitment to 'the inviolability of a
minimum extent of individual liberty entails some such absolute stand' to, for instance, natural law, utility, rights, the word
of God, or the permanent interests of man.[40] For Strauss and
other critics, the dilemma of modern liberalism derives from
the fact that it 'cannot live without an absolute basis and cannot
live with an absolute basis'.[41]

In a similar manner, Michael Sandel argued that although
one might say that Berlin is 'not strictly speaking a relativist
– he affirms the ideal of freedom of choice – his position comes
perilously close to foundering on the relativist predicament'.[42]
Berlin's response is to deny that pluralism implies scepticism

or relativism. He argues that: 'Principles are not less sacred because their duration cannot be guaranteed. Indeed the very desire for guarantees that our values are eternal and secure in some objective heaven is perhaps only a craving for the certainties of childhood or the absolute values of our primitive past.' Quoting Schumpeter, he continues: 'To realize the relative validity of one's convictions . . . and yet stand for them unflinchingly, is what distinguishes a civilised man from a barbarian.' Further, to 'demand more than this is perhaps a deep and incurable metaphysical need; but to allow it to determine one's practice is a symptom of an equally deep, and more dangerous, moral and political immaturity'.[43]

The rhetorical force of this statement is typical in the way in which Berlin's endorsement of the idea of pluralism is connected to a particular vision of the good, civilized, society in which morally 'mature' individuals can flourish. But, as Sandel and other critics have argued, this idea of Berlin's is far from clear:[44]

> If one's convictions are only relatively valid, why stand for them unflinchingly? In a tragically-configured moral universe, such as Berlin assumes, is the ideal of freedom any less subject than competing ideals to the ultimate incommensurability of values? If so, in what can its privileged status consist? And if freedom has no morally privileged status, if it is just one value among many, then what can be said for liberalism?

Similarly, Sandel and others have argued that if Berlin is to convince us, then:

> both the nature of the convictions and what is done to uphold them must matter. Otherwise, might not a Caligula or a Goebbels qualify as civilized rather than barbarian? It is equally unclear why we should be so presumptuous as to label as 'barbarian' the vast majority of human beings who believe their convictions to be fully valid or whose stance, regardless of whether or not they do, is less than flinching.

Drawing upon the same intuitions, Rorty defended Berlin's account against Sandel's criticism. He insisted that the problem in both Sandel's and Berlin's work is that they are still, in one way or another, working with a vocabulary which is permeated

with Enlightenment preconceptions. Berlin, from Rorty's point
of view, ought to simply give up worrying whether pluralism
could be distinguished from relativism. A liberal culture, as
envisioned by Rorty, would simply 'not assume that a form of
cultural life is no stronger than its philosophical foundations'.[45]
John Gray has endorsed this 'historicist' interpretation of
Berlin's pluralism. Although Berlin does not take his thought
in this direction, Gray argues that this is the most convincing
way of making sense of his version of pluralism.[46] Nevertheless,
it is clear that Berlin would not be convinced by Rorty's relaxed
pragmatism.

Berlin denied that his pluralism cannot be distinguished
from relativism. He argued that the doctrines of theorists such
as Strauss, when taken to their logical conclusion, offer a clear
example of the fallacy of the idea, that he so strongly opposed,
of monism in political and moral thought. The basic fallacy
here, in Berlin's view, is that Strauss and his followers:

> appear to believe in absolute good and evil, right and wrong,
> directly perceived by means of an *a priori* vision, a metaphysical
> eye-by use of a Platonic rational faculty which has not been
> granted to me. Plato, Aristotle, the Bible, the Talmud,
> Maimonides, perhaps Aquinas, and other Scholastics of the
> Middle Ages, knew what was the best life for me. So did he,
> and his disciples claim this today. I am not so privileged.[47]

In response to criticism, Berlin sought to clarify what he saw
as the difference between pluralism and relativism. For
example, looking at the 'alleged relativism in eighteenth-
century thought', Berlin sought to revise the impression that
he might have given in his earlier discussion of the pivotal role
of Vico and Herder in the development of both western and
his own political thought. The importance of Vico and Herder
derives, in part, from what Berlin sees as their attack upon the
view of Enlightenment thinkers such as Hume and Diderot
that human nature is essentially the same for all societies
throughout history and that the application of a uniform
human reason was sufficient to establish the truth about the
best form of political community. This criticism of these central
ideas of the Enlightenment was bound to lead to the accusation
of relativism.[48]

In order to counter this charge, Berlin points out that it is important to distinguish two types of relativism. Relativism concerning judgements of fact must be distinguished from relativism concerning judgements of value. The first kind of relativism is that which denies the possibility of any kind of objective knowledge. It does this by arguing that the social location of the inquirer is bound to systematically distort or bias his or her investigations. This version of the sociology of knowledge, especially in its 'total' or hard version, is bound to be self-refuting. Berlin does not enter into the detailed debate about the claims of such a position. He takes it to be an attitude which is largely a development of nineteenth-century German Romantic irrationalism as well as of the theories of Hegel and Marx, which, although confused, have had a pervasive influence upon much modern political and social thought.[49]

The real problem that Berlin had to confront was that of value relativism. What does Berlin mean by relativism? He states that he 'takes it to mean a doctrine according to which the judgement of a man or group, since it is the expression or statement of a taste, or emotional attitude or outlook, is simply what it is, with no objective correlate which determines its truth or falsehood'. Or, put in another way, 'I prefer coffee, you prefer champagne. We have different tastes. There is no more to be said.' Relativism amounts to the idea that each culture is 'enclosed in its own impenetrable bubble' which makes true understanding or communication between different cultures as carriers of diverse values impossible.[50]

At the centre of Berlin's account of pluralism is the claim that incommensurability does not entail relativism. Pluralism, for Berlin, is essentially a theory of the incommensurability of values. Nevertheless, developing his interpretation of Vico and Herder, Berlin argues that although they were right to recognize the incommensurability of values that cultural diversity seems to imply, this was not taken by them to mean that such diversity or pluralism is an insurmountable barrier to understanding; nor does it license an irrational relativism. When Vico and Herder point to the need to see the beliefs of other societies in their true context, they are:

> not telling us that the values of these societies, dissimilar to ours, cast doubts on the objectivity of our own, or are

undermined by them, because the existence of conflicting or incompatible outlooks must mean that at most only one of these is valid, the rest being false; or, alternatively, that none belong to the kind of judgements that can be considered either valid or invalid.[51]

Even if we accept Berlin's argument that pluralism does not necessarily lead to relativism because it would not rule out the possibility of understanding and criticizing other value standpoints, it still seems that some troubling questions have not disappeared. A central problem here is embedded in his interpretation of the history of western ideas and this, as a consequence, haunts his account of pluralism. Central to Berlin's interpretation of western thought is the idea that the 'romantic revolution' was its 'greatest turning point'. The significance of Romanticism for political thought rests on the idea that, in Berlin's view, it initiated 'the destruction of the notion of truth and validity in ethics and politics, not merely objective or absolute truth, but subjective and relative truth also – truth and validity as such – with vast and indeed incalculable results'.[52]

The Romantic revolution produced 'a reversal of values'. It proposed that:

> man has no identifiable nature, whether static or dynamic, for he creates himself: he creates his own values, and thereby transforms himself, and the transformed self creates new values, so that we cannot *ex hypothesi* ever tell what the upshot will be of his attempt to realize them; for he can only attempt – he cannot be answerable for the consequences, or know whether he will succeed or not . . . since his values are not discovered but created, no system of propositions can be constructed to describe them, for they are not facts, not entities in the world; they are not there to be identified and labelled by a science of ethics or politics, whether empirically or a priori. Finally, there is no guarantee that the values of different civilizations, or nations, or individuals, will necessarily harmonize.[53]

The form of pluralism produced by this intellectual revolution was such that it naturally led to a scepticism concerning the nature of all value judgements. Berlin strenuously denies this inference. 'Do we truly believe that value judgements are not judgements at all, but arbitrary acts of self-commitment? Do we believe that the sciences of man are irrelevant to political purposes, that anthropology, psychology, sociology, can instruct us only about means, about techniques?'[54]

The central problem that Berlin's pluralism faces here is that of the rational irresolvability of value conflicts. The curious tension at the heart of Berlin's thought derives from the way in which he is both committed to a defence of the ideals of the Enlightenment and of liberalism, while, at the same time, he is equally impressed by the criticisms made by the Romantic counter-Enlightenment. Berlin's own interpretation and fascination with the counter-Enlightenment has puzzled many commentators. Indeed, it can be argued that Berlin's way of opposing en bloc an abstract concept of the Enlightenment against an equally abstract concept of the counter-Enlightenment has led him to 'go native'. Berlin, it is argued, has become so involved with enlisting the thinkers of the counter-Enlightenment into the services of pluralism that he has progressively lost sight of what it was the 'counter' to. Berlin has implicitly adopted the counter-Enlightenment's caricature of what it was reacting against. The question which this leads to is whether Berlin's adoption of the idea of pluralism, essentially derived from counter-Enlightenment thought, potentially undermines his commitment to the ideals of the Enlightenment and of liberalism. Perhaps the best way to see this facet of Berlin's thought is to recognize that 'Berlin is an ultra-liberal frustrated by the limits of the Enlightenment itself'.[55]

What is the rational response to the problem of plural and conflicting values? Berlin has approached this question from several directions. If values do collide, how are we to choose between them? This is the difficult question that Berlin had to answer in order to clarify the distinction between pluralism and relativism. The problem of the conflict between incommensurable values is evident in the concluding passages of Berlin's 'Two Concepts of Liberty'. Here we see very clearly the tension that many of Berlin's critics see as the source of what appears to be an insoluble problem when expressed in these terms. On the one hand, we are presented with the picture of a world of plural and conflicting values. The conflict between negative and positive conceptions of liberty is presented as clear evidence of the 'fact of pluralism'. The world in which we live 'is one in which we are faced with choices between ends equally ultimate, and claims equally absolute, the realization of some of which must inevitably involve the sacrifice of others'. It follows from this, in Berlin's view, that we cannot escape 'the agony and necessity of choice' and it is this that gives value to political freedom conceived as negative liberty. This is, in turn, linked to an attack upon the idea that there could be 'some single formula' in terms of which 'the diverse ends of men can be harmoniously realized'. This claim does not, in itself, contribute to the argument for pluralism. It should be understood, in effect, as an essential component of Berlin's defence of the value of political liberty. Furthermore, Berlin's account of value pluralism implies that those who do not experience or who reject the idea that there are such value conflicts are themselves somewhat deficient as human beings. He asserts that these

> collisions of values are of the essence of what they are and what we are. If we are told that these contradictions will be solved in some perfect world in which all good things can be harmonized in principle, then we must answer, to those who say this, that the meanings they attach to the names which for us denote the conflicting values are not ours. We must say that the world in which what we see as incompatible values are not in conflict is a world altogether beyond our ken; that principles which are harmonized in this other world are not the principles with which, in our daily lives, we are acquainted; if they are transformed, it is into conceptions not known to us on earth.[56]

According to Berlin, if we are to act in a politically mature manner, we must both recognize the 'relative validity' of our convictions and be prepared to stand by them 'unflinchingly'.

Berlin seems to take two positions concerning the way in which we are to cope with a world of plural and conflicting values. He argues that, as a consequence of our recognition of the permanence of plural and conflicting values, we must be prepared to choose between irreconcilable and conflicting values. However, at the same time, Berlin seeks to limit the scope of this pluralism. Although there are no 'final guarantees', Berlin's political thought does, in fact, rest upon an idea of universal human nature. It is this idea which sets the limits to his pluralism and which prevents the possibility of a total incommensurability of values. It is this notion of a common

human nature which makes cross-cultural understanding possible. Berlin makes use here of the image of a 'bridgehead'. He
states that communication between cultures is only possible
'because what makes men human is common to them, and acts
as a bridge between them'.[57]

Berlin's political thought rests on a 'philosophical anthropology' in the sense of a hybrid constructed from the human
sciences and the philosophy of mind. This form of philosophical anthropology does not necessarily imply an essentialist or
absolutist view of human character, but is to be understood in
the sense that 'the commonality of human nature is to be found
in the mode of explanation to which we are all susceptible'.[58]
For Berlin, when the great political philosophers of the past
disagree with each other:

> they are not complaining merely of empirical ignorance or poor
> logic or insufficient experimental evidence, or internal incoher-
> ence. They denounce their adversaries mainly for not under-
> standing what men are and what relationships between them
> – or between them and outside forces – make them men; they
> complain of blindness not to those transient characteristics of
> such relations, but to those constant characteristics (such as
> discrimination of right from good for Kant, or, for Marx, sys-
> tematic self-transmutation by their own labour) that they
> regard as fundamental to the notion of man as such.

This points, in Berlin's view, to the existence of a 'permanent
framework in terms of which, and not about which, ordinary
empirical disagreements can arise'.[59] This idea of 'a permanent
framework' has itself operated as a limiting concept throughout the development of Berlin's political thought. It is not an
idea, as some critics have argued, which Berlin introduced into
his later work in order to block 'the path from the liberal notion
of pluralism to the nihilist consequence of relativism'.[60]

Berlin's account of the limits to relativism rests to a large
extent upon the supposition that we must accept that, despite
the unavoidable clash of plural values, the moral universe has
a relatively stable and permanent core. This is, itself, best identified in terms of those features, motives and reasons, which
we refer to when trying to explain and justify human conduct.
The permanence of politics and, hence, the need for political
philosophy, rests upon the fact that our 'political categories

(and values) are themselves part of this all but inescapable web of ways of living, acting and thinking, a network liable to change only as a result of radical changes in reality, or through dissociation from reality on the part of individuals, that is to say, madness'.[61]

What bearing does this conception of the underlying structure of concepts and categories have upon the question of the rationality of values and of value judgements? Berlin's view of value pluralism is such that 'the old perennial belief in the possibility of realizing ultimate harmony is a fallacy'. Berlin takes the collision of the 'Great Goods' to mean that 'human creativity may depend upon a variety of mutually exclusive choices'.[62] Berlin seems to waver in his response to this question. He states that, if we accept his version of pluralism, then we have no alternative but to say that 'men choose between ultimate values' but 'they choose as they do, because their life and thought are determined by fundamental moral categories and concepts that are, at any rate over large stretches of time and space, a part of their being and thought and sense of their own identity; part of what makes them human'.[63] In another formulation, Berlin states that if we ask the question 'How do we choose between possibilities?', then there seems to be no clear answer. Nevertheless, the collisions of value, it is now argued, can at least be 'softened' even if they cannot be avoided[64]

> Claims can be balanced, compromises can be reached: in concrete situations not every claim is of equal force – so much liberty and so much equality; so much for sharp moral condemnation, and so much for understanding a given human situation; so much for the full force of the law, and so much for the prerogative of mercy; for feeding the hungry, clothing the naked, healing the sick, sheltering the homeless. Priorities, never final and absolute, must be established.

In other words, Berlin admits to the possibility of trade-offs as well as sacrifices between competing values. This way of avoiding a dramatizing of the conflict of values coheres with Berlin's belief that there is also a large area of agreement among peoples at different times and in different places.

Nevertheless, Berlin's way of stating the problem in the language of choice and decision seems to lead him towards a kind of existentialist stance. Considering ultimate values, those values which are regarded as ends in themselves and not as means to other ends, we can do nothing other than commit ourselves. The problem here is that the choice itself seems to resist, according to this way of posing the question, any kind of rational foundation. If this is so, then it is difficult to see how Berlin would distinguish his position from that of other theorists, such as Max Weber and Carl Schmitt, who, equally stressing the reality of decision in the context of an unavoidable pluralism of values, have derived very different political conclusions from it.[65]

The difficulties involved in deciphering Berlin's position on this question derive from a tension that is embedded within his political thought. Berlin is essentially committed to the values of the Enlightenment, but, at the same time, he has been himself deeply influenced by the thinkers of the counter-Enlightenment. There is, throughout Berlin's work, an unresolved tension between the ideas of the Enlightenment and those of the counter-Enlightenment. This tension shows itself, to a certain extent, in the way in which Berlin is sometimes guilty of exaggerating the internal historical and philosophical unity of these two movements of ideas.

Berlin has argued persuasively that the most significant turning point in the history of western political thought was the development, mainly in Germany, during the eighteenth and nineteenth centuries of Romanticism. Nevertheless, Berlin argues that this profound transformation was not decisive. The 'older morality' represented by such diverse thinkers as Aristotle, the utilitarians, Hume, Montesquieu and Herder, which 'judged the acts of men', to a large degree, in terms of their consequences 'did not go under before this revolutionary wave'. In the light of these assertions, Berlin draws back from whatever relativistic or irrational implications we might want to infer. If we ask the question whether or not it makes sense to talk of the rationality of value judgements, Berlin's answer is equivocal. According to Berlin, our predicament owes its character to the fact that we are the heirs of two conflicting traditions. Modern political thought contains within itself intellectual and moral commitments that derive from both the Enlightenment and the Romantic counter-Enlightenment. This duality of influences is correspondingly shown in the persistent tension between an emphasis upon either the morality of motive or the morality of consequences.[66]

Berlin's pluralism has aimed at disconnecting the defence of liberalism from a naive belief in progress and human perfectibility. Nevertheless, the precise nature of the connection between liberalism and pluralism, according to Berlin, is not clear. Clearly, Berlin believes that liberalism gains a more secure backing, 'a sense of reality', if it recognizes the significance of pluralism. However, Berlin is also clear that the two concepts are not to be confused. He states that they 'are not the same or even overlapping concepts. There are liberal theories which are not pluralistic. I believe in both liberalism and pluralism, but they are not logically connected.'[67]

This remark seems to support the argument that there is, contrary to what Berlin has on other occasions also implied, not only no strong or logical connection between pluralism and liberalism but, instead, a sharp contradiction between them. It can be argued, for example, that pluralism 'tells us that we must choose but not what to choose'. There is a troubling possibility that the idea that pluralism undermines both the Enlightenment belief in the power of reason and the claims of liberalism is the correct implication of Berlin's argument. If this is so, then liberalism must be perceived for what it really is: no more and no less than a groundless and local political ideal.

At the root of the argument that liberalism is undermined by pluralism is an argument to the effect that conflicting and incommensurable values are, often, beyond the scope of rational comparison. Although Berlin sometimes seems to imply this, such a conclusion is not the view that predominates in his work. Pluralism, it turns out, is not always so difficult to live with. In fact, Berlin's characterization of thinkers as being either 'hedgehogs' or 'foxes' has led some to apply the former label to Berlin himself. While it is tempting to say that Berlin is a hedgehog and that his big idea is pluralism, this could also lead an interpretation in the wrong direction. Attributing the characteristics of the hedgehog to Berlin might lead one to imply the existence of a system, which is not really there or meant to be there, within Berlin's writings. It is easy to overlook the obvious fact that Berlin's style is that of the essayist. He has approached a set of related questions from different angles without the desire to construct a philosophical system.

Instead, his work exemplifies the tensions and lack of water-tight logical connections that are bound to be a feature of this style of political writing. Berlin's style can lead to confusions of 'voice'. It is not always clear who is speaking: is it Berlin or the thinker whose thought he is interpreting?[68]

The question of foxes and hedgehogs is not as straightforward as it looks at first glance. If Berlin was a fox, then we could ask 'what kind of fox'? There is more than one type of fox and more than one type of hedgehog. Following Stephen Lukes's suggestion, we can recognize the existence of a typology of hedgehogs and foxes. He lists positivist hedgehogs such as Comte and, controversially according to Berlin, Marx; universalist or uniformitarian hedgehogs such as Hume, Locke and Voltaire; rationalist hedgehogs such as Condorcet; and monist hedgehogs such as the Philosophes.[69] All of these forms of hedgehog-ism have been opposed by the thinkers whom Berlin has found interesting, and, among those, the most interesting were those whom he saw as the precursors of his own brand of pluralism. Clearly, there were foxes with whom Berlin was sympathetic and those whose ideas he opposed. While Berlin found the ideas of a diverse group of foxes, including Vico, Hamann, de Maistre, J. S. Mill, Sorel and Herzen, as interesting and important, he clearly had no sympathy with some other influential foxes, such as Nietzsche and those post-modernists who have been influenced by him. Perhaps the at times confusing distinction between foxes and hedgehogs is an example of the use of 'gross concepts'. The difficulty of placing thinkers, including Berlin himself, straightforwardly into one or the other of these categories may be a reflection of the fact that it might make more sense to think of these concepts in relational rather than in stark oppositional terms. It would then be a question of the relative weight of fox-like or hedgehog-like ideas within the work of a particular political thinker.[70]

Michael Walzer has pointed to a way of answering the question concerning the relationship between liberalism and pluralism that seems to cohere with Berlin's intentions. He argues that, rather than looking for a logical connection or lack of one between pluralism and liberalism, it is more useful to think in a more informal style and simply 'stress the many obvious and ordinary connections' between them.[71] Berlin and Bernard Williams have, in fact, argued in this way. They point out that

there are many possible kinds of relationship between pluralism and liberalism. This answer, however, seems to be anoma-
lous within the broader context of Berlin's work.[72]

If we ask whether pluralism entails liberalism, then the
answer seems to be that it does not in any clear-cut sense.
Instead, it might be more useful to start from a commitment
to liberalism and ask how it coheres with pluralism. Walzer,
for example, has pointed out there are many liberals who are
not pluralists but very few contemporary value pluralists who
are not liberals. It is difficult to see how anyone would accept
value pluralism if they were not already receptive to liberal
ideas. Put in this way, perhaps there is an irresolvable tension
in Berlin's pluralism. If value pluralism is true and only liberal-
minded people can recognize this truth, then liberalism may
itself have a peculiar status. Furthermore, there is an additional
problem. Value pluralism is itself a controversial philosophical
doctrine. As Berlin himself points out, despite the enormous
amount of attention devoted to it in recent political theory, it
still seems to be a minority view in western culture. If liberalism is based upon the controversial doctrine of value pluralism,
then it is difficult to see how it can avoid itself being 'one more
partisan ideal'.[73]

The post-Berlinian discovery of the significance of pluralism
is in many ways a repetition or rediscovery, rarely acknowledged, of Max Weber's reflections on modernity. The vision of
value pluralism that Berlin argued for is one that bears the
imprint of the time in which it was formulated. For Berlin, it
was clear that the argument for pluralism had an anti-totalitarian political message. This is more than apparent in the way
in which he connected this topic with the argument that
monism, the opposite of pluralism, had been responsible for
the 'slaughter of individuals on the altars of the great historical
ideals – justice or progress or the happiness of future genera-
tions, or the sacred mission or emancipation of a nation or race
or class, or even liberty itself, which demands the sacrifice of
individuals for the freedom of society'.[74] Berlin's account of
value pluralism appeals to our 'ordinary experience' which, for
him, is grounded in reflection upon history and, especially, the
horrors of the twentieth century. This is sufficient evidence
that the 'world that we encounter in ordinary experience is one
in which we are faced with choices between ends equally ulti-

mate, and claims equally absolute, the realisation of some of which must inevitably involve the sacrifice of others'.[75] It is clear that an important rhetorical component of Berlin's advocacy of pluralism is a powerful anti-utopianism, conceived against the background of the Cold War.[76] Berlin's advocacy of the benefits of pluralism and his defence of liberalism has much in common with other liberal thinkers of that period, such as Karl Popper, Friedrich von Hayek and Jacob Talmon.[77] The concern to get the anti-totalitarian message across is one possible reason why there is one large gap in Berlin's account of pluralism. Despite the attractive plausibility of his account, there is a marked lack of detailed argument. For example, at no point does Berlin explain exactly why a belief in monism must lead to tyranny or worse, or why a belief in pluralism necessarily is a protection against these dangers.[78]

Given the centrality of the idea of pluralism in Berlin's thought, and his deep and extensive knowledge of the history of political ideas, it is odd that there are very few references to Max Weber in his work. Berlin confessed in an interview that when 'I first formulated this idea, which is a long time ago, I'd never read a page of Weber. I had no idea that he said these things. People often ask me, but surely Weber was the first person to say this. I answer that I am sure he is, but I had no idea of it.'[79] One can excuse Berlin's lapse of memory here, but he seems on other occasions to have shown more awareness of Weber's work than he was prepared to admit. For instance, in his introduction to the famous essay on liberty, Berlin remarks in a footnote that 'the classical – and still, it seems to me, the best – exposition of this state of mind [i.e., pluralism] is to be found in Max Weber's distinction between the ethics of conscience and the ethics of responsibility in "Politics as a Vocation"'.[80] One possible reason for Berlin's failure to publicly pay sufficient attention to Weber's work was his general disapproval of the intellectual claims of sociology (and this was a common view for many of his generation in British intellectual life). As far as Berlin was concerned, Weber was a sociologist and most of contemporary sociology was to be condemned as a pseudo-scientific distraction from political philosophy and the history of ideas. When questioned about the work of Raymond Aron, a fellow liberal political thinker (and sociologist) of the same generation, Berlin states that although he found some of Aron's work to be of great value, he could not say the same about his early works on the German philosophy of history and sociology. Nevertheless, Berlin does bring himself to say that he 'never read much Weber, one of my great deficiencies, which I could remedy but never have. I have never ceased to lament not reading enough Max Weber.'[81] This is an interesting and revealing comment in light of the fact that Aron was also struggling to come to terms with the challenge that Weber's value pluralism offers to much of the orthodoxy of contemporary political thinking.[82]

In a similar fashion, John Gray has recognized there is a case for seeing 'a more plausible affinity' between the ideas of Weber and Berlin. Unfortunately, however, he argues that Weber failed to provide 'any account of the sources of such clashes [of values] in moral psychology, in philosophical anthropology, or in conflict between different cultural forms'.[83] This outrageous view has been criticized by Ernest Gellner. He pointed out that this is one of 'the most bizarre charges ever made'. Weber's 'justified fame rests precisely on the unrivalled richness of his exploration of different cultural forms, which underly the diversity of values. He didn't merely talk about warring gods, he explored them with unequalled depth.'[84]

It is also worth mentioning that Berlin was aware of the work of Leo Strauss. This is significant because a central component of Strauss's political thought consists of a dialogue with Weber's value pluralism. In Strauss's view, this is a dangerous form of value relativism.[85] Strauss accepted that no one 'since Weber has devoted a comparable amount of intelligence, assiduity, and almost fanatical devotion to the basic problem of the social sciences. Whatever may have been his errors, he is the greatest social scientist of our century.'[86] However, the problem for Strauss was that Weber's account of value pluralism was a symptom of what he saw as the crisis of German 'historicism'. The problem with historicism, as far as Strauss was concerned, was that it led to a rejection of the classical tradition of political philosophy which itself was founded upon a doctrine of natural right. If natural right is rejected, 'not only because all human thought is held to be historical but likewise because it is thought that there is a variety of unchangeable principles of right or of goodness which conflict with one another, and none of which can be proved to be superior to the others', we are inescapably led towards nihilism.

Strauss pointed out there are two striking facts concerning Weber's reflections on the nature of the social sciences. One is that Weber spends, throughout his whole work, hardly more than thirty pages discussing the basis of his position on the nature of value pluralism. The other relevant fact is that, as Weber himself indicates, 'his thesis was only the generalized version of an older and more common view, namely, that the conflict between ethics and politics is insoluble: political action is sometimes impossible without incurring moral guilt'.[87] Weber's account of value pluralism, as far as Strauss was concerned, rested upon an acceptance of a view of human life in which there is no solution to the conflict between values. The insoluble conflict of values itself is 'a part, or a consequence of the comprehensive view according to which human life is essentially an inescapable conflict'.[88] Peace, on this account, is either unachievable or undesirable. It is unachievable simply because conflict and its inevitability form one of the basic presuppositions of Weber's political thought. It is undesirable because a 'perpetual peace' is incompatible with a truly human existence. It would create the conditions for the rule of 'the last men who have invented happiness'.[89]

Berlin, in an interview, demonstrates the difference in viewpoints here. He makes it quite clear that he has no sympathy for Strauss's critique of modernity. Strauss and his followers are guilty of believing in:

> eternal, immutable, absolute values, true for all men everywhere at all times, God-given Natural Law and the like . . . He and they appear to me to believe in absolute good and evil, right and wrong, directly perceived by means of a kind of a priori vision, a metaphysical eye – by the use of a Platonic rational faculty which has not been granted to me.[90]

Strauss, in turn, found in Berlin's version of pluralism all the dangers and confusions that characterize modern political thought. The problem with Berlin's account, according to Strauss, is that his attempt to combine pluralism with liberalism 'cannot live without an absolute basis and cannot live with an absolute basis'.[91] Strauss's argument is that, although Berlin's essay on liberty might provide a useful 'anticommunist manifesto', the theoretical failure of his pluralism is clear. The difficulty is that Berlin wants to say both that there are two equally valid forms of liberty, positive and negative, but in defence of liberalism he favours the second. He can only do this by introducing a notion of the 'absoluteness' or 'sacred' character of the distinction between the two values of positive and negative liberty. Berlin's and, by implication, all forms of pluralism cannot avoid the relativist predicament. Strauss's criticism of Berlin and of Weber has to be understood in terms of his desire to avoid 'the Weimar problem'. It was his view that the idea that the world is constituted by a plurality of values which are in conflict with each other, none of which can be shown to be superior to the others, was a fundamental cause of the downfall of the Weimar Republic. It is a curious fact that much of contemporary political philosophy still operates in the shadow of the ideological debates of Weimar Germany.[92]

In order to attempt to escape the predicament that Strauss outlines, Berlin oscillates between two positions. On the one hand, he states that, supervenient upon the plurality of political and moral values, we have to assert there is, indeed, a permanent and stable core. In fact, he finds himself defending 'the kernel of truth in the old a priori Natural Law doctrines'.[93] Reflecting upon the lessons to be learnt from the European wars of the twentieth century, Berlin rejected what he saw as the existentialist and extremist argument that 'there are no human values, still less European values'. Our reaction to the 'excesses of totalitarianism' have shown us that this is not a valid diagnosis. In response, Berlin argued that the pluralism of values he has defended also has to admit the presence of 'a scale of values by which the majority of mankind – and in particular western Europeans – in fact live, . . . as part of what in their moments of self-awareness constitutes for them the essential nature of man'.[94]

However, at other times Berlin accepts that, for the individual, ultimately one just has to take sides, to decide for one value rather than another. This is a problem for Berlin insofar as he wants to combine his concept of pluralism with a defence of liberalism. The question that arises is this: if liberty is just one value among others, why give it priority? The relativist predicament can only be avoided if we recognize that 'some values – however general and however few – enter into the normal definition of what constitutes a sane human being . . . In this sense, then, pursuit of, or failure to pursue, certain ends can be regarded as evidence of – and in extreme cases part of the definition of – irrationality.'[95] However, in the eyes of his critics, this seems to get us no further. The relativist predicament has not been avoided. 'In a tragically-configured moral universe, such as Berlin assumes, is the ideal of freedom any less subject than competing ideals to the ultimate incommensurability of values?'[96]

Although Isaiah Berlin is usually credited with the introduction of the idea of value pluralism into modern political thought, it is clear that the idea was not as original as Berlin sometimes seemed to want us to believe. Certainly, the concept of value pluralism appears to have been discussed in some detail by American pragmatists, and it is hard to believe that Berlin was unaware of this fact.[97] However, the most glaring omission occurs in Berlin's failure to acknowledge that Max Weber had put forward an account of value pluralism that was both influential and impressive. It is generally acknowledged that it is in Max Weber's work that we find one of the most powerful assertions of the more existential or radical versions of the thesis of value pluralism. Nevertheless, Weber would probably have some sympathy with Berlin's predicament of wanting to defend pluralism while avoiding the dangers of nihilism and relativism.

Critics of Berlin have noted that his version of pluralism is unconvincing in its attempt to evade the agonistic nature of the polytheism that Weber stressed.[98] Berlin's attempt to come to terms with pluralism and to make it compatible with liberalism marks the outer limits of a political theory that denies the politically pessimistic conclusions that Weber drew, while not venturing into the more systematic style of theorizing represented by the work of John Rawls. Berlin's political thought does not succumb to the despair that can so easily accompany Weber's more sombre vision. At the same time, it is deeply sceptical of any attempt to construct an escape from the dilemmas of pluralism founded upon a belief that a rational philosophical method can enable us to transcend the clash of political ideas and values.

3 Stuart Hampshire: Pluralism and Pessimism

Stuart Hampshire's work on moral and political philosophy is
an important and distinctive reflection upon the nature and
permanence of plural and conflicting values in human affairs.
Hampshire has put forward a version of the idea of value pluralism that differs in important ways from the ideas of his
one-time colleague Isaiah Berlin.[99] In doing so, Hampshire has
illuminated our understanding of the nature of political thinking in the modern world. Although Hampshire is well known
for his work in the philosophy of mind and action, his work
in political and moral theory has, unjustly, not received the
same degree of attention.[100] Hampshire's political thought is of
great importance because it offers a sophisticated and challenging blend of pluralism and pessimism. He states, characteristically, that it is his reflections on pluralism that confirm his
pessimism.[101]

As with Berlin, it is the experience of totalitarianism and
the political disasters of the twentieth century that provided
the main context for reflection on the meaning of pluralism.
While it is Soviet communism that is explicitly targeted by
Berlin's pluralism, Hampshire focuses upon the political and
moral significance of the Nazi regime.

The success of the Nazi movement, in Hampshire's eyes,
ought to have ended the innocence that is exemplified in the
central tradition of academic moral philosophy that extends
from Hume through to Mill, Sidgewick and Moore. Their
innocence was expressed in the assumption that 'it was sufficient to establish some truths about the great goods for
mankind, and then deduce from these truths the necessary
human virtues and vices and the necessary social policies'.[102]
Interestingly, Hampshire's account of the problem of evil finds
an echo in the later work of John Rawls where he explicitly
refers to the 'underlying thoughts and attitudes about the world
as a whole' that reflect upon the way in which we think about
questions of politics and philosophy. In this particular case,
Rawls refers to Carl Schmitt, 'the manic evil of the Holocaust',
and the collapse of faith in the possibility of a just and democratic society in Weimar Germany.

Hampshire's idea of pluralism is founded on the observation
that the origin of morality ought to be understood against the

background of our common experience of conflicts of aims and of purpose. According to Hampshire, all philosophical attempts, from Plato onwards, to eliminate or to control such conflicts by showing that they are only illusory ought to be rejected. Any idea that moral codes and moral conflicts are to be seen as, in reality, forming part of a coherent system ought to be treated, similarly, with scepticism. As with Isaiah Berlin, the argument here is against the thought of 'any ideal of rationality for practical reason that entails the softening or elimination of ultimate conflicts'.[103] Unavoidable conflict rather than ultimate harmony is to be expected in human affairs. Put in its most basic terms, Hampshire's argument rests upon the idea that: 'the capacity to think scatters a range of differences and conflicts before us: different languages, different ways of life, different specializations of aim within a way of life, different conventions and styles also within a shared way of life, different prohibitions'.[104] The activity of human thinking has an essentially reflexive and imaginative character, and it is this that provides the foundation for his argument for the persistence of pluralism and conflict.

Hampshire's account of the nature of pluralism has been advanced against the background of an analysis of some commonly held beliefs about reason and rationality. He argues there is a fundamental misunderstanding, deeply embedded in western thought, that can be traced back to the philosophy of Plato and Aristotle. The central idea of the divided soul that we find in their thought is, in Hampshire's view, a principle source of their and our intellectual difficulties. In particular, the claim that reason is the ruling part or highest element in the soul is, therefore, made to reflect and to be a reflection of the ideal polis. This is an idea that we do not need to accept.

Hampshire offers an alternative to the aristocratic model of the mind advocated by Plato, Aristotle and the ancients. In direct contrast to their preferred imagery, he proposes that the practice of public debate is a more appropriate model for thinking about the workings of the human mind. The image of the council chamber is proposed as an appropriate way of thinking about the operation of practical reason. In other words, although he is critical of Aristotle's hierarchical image of the soul, Hampshire adopts his deliberative conception of practical reason. This idea has survived since Aristotle proposed it, Hampshire argues, for good reasons. In his view, it is a basic and general fact of human social life that 'issues of policy will be debated in some assembly of chosen persons, whether a democratically or aristocratically chosen assembly, or an assembly chosen simply by a monarch or tyrant. The institution of articulating and reviewing contrary opinions is of necessity species-wide.'[105]

Hampshire contrasts the plurality of concepts of the good with the idea of a universal conception of justice as a minimum moral requirement. But the same cannot be said for any particular conception of the good. He argues that 'as a lesson of recent history' we know now 'that those theorists who have in the past represented respect for justice as a necessary and universal requirement of any morality were right. If this barrier against the drive to domination, and against overwhelming ambition is subverted, we are in a moral desert, where there are no limits and nothing is forbidden in the pursuit of power'.[106]

Hampshire argues for a strong version of pluralism. In contrast to Berlin and other contemporary theorists who stress the unavoidable plurality of values, Hampshire argues that his slogan that 'all determination is negation' presents a much stronger thesis.[107] Rather than arguing the case for the historical reality of moral pluralism, Hampshire is concerned to point out there is a simple truth that has to be recognized. It is in the nature of visions of the good to define themselves, to a large degree, in terms of their rejection of rivals. As a consequence, moral pluralism is an inevitable though not necessarily constant element of human experience.

The foundation of Hampshire's account has two sources: a conception of the nature of individuality and a view of the nature of the relationship between political theory, historical experience and the theory of knowledge. The first conception can be approached in several ways. Hampshire does not see moral pluralism as having a particularly modern provenance. If the nature of pluralism is as Hampshire says it is, then it cannot be a definitive symptom of western modernity. In contrast to Berlin, for example, who generally takes pluralism to have a specifically modern character, Hampshire points to the way in which the reality of plural and conflicting values is built into the structure of human experience. If we recognize fully the reflexive element in practical reason, then, Hampshire argues, the Greek distinction between nature and convention points to an unavoidable duality. 'The distinguishing capacity for thought, which for Aristotle opened the way to a rational choice between kinds of life and kinds of human excellence, at the same time complicates and multiplies choice, and, more important, puts a limit on its rationality'.

Although some conceptions of the good might claim that they legislate for the whole of mankind, while others will be of more local importance, Hampshire insists there is one universal moral requirement that applies to all conceptions of the good. This is the claim that every person forms through experience some conception of the good that they are prepared to defend. This has to be understood as a potentiality, although it is not always realized. Nevertheless, this potential for individuals to develop their own conceptions of the good, based, to a large degree, upon their own unique memories, creates an irreducible diversity. No sufficient reasons could ever be given 'for taking one end, such as the general happiness or the exercise of reason, as the single supreme end'. Just as it is in human nature to speak a variety of natural languages, it is also part of that nature to 'develop idiosyncrasies of style and of imagination, and to form specific conceptions of the good'.

Hampshire also takes it as a central component of human nature that we can understand the universal languages of logic and mathematics and can respond to ideas of fairness and of procedural justice even if we attach different substantive conceptions to these ideas. Hampshire's argument here turns on the requirement that the very diversity of conceptions of the good produces the virtue of fairness. The argument states it is a requirement that a degree of basic fairness in negotiation provides:

> the ground for a shared negative morality independent of specific conceptions of the good: this is the common decency, which moral and religious fanatics try to undermine in the name of their particular conception of substantial justice, derived from their particular conception of the good. The great evil is the destruction of respect for generally recognized fair procedures adjudicating and compromising, procedures which which have been built up over time out of earlier recognized procedures, and which are always capable of being reformed.

Just as theoretical reason, being a species-wide and cross-cultural endowment, is at home with logic and mathematics, practical reason, is at home with the weighing of alternatives, with judgement and with compromise.[108]

The problem here is that this analysis begs the question of the explanation of the value of individuality. Why do we, in Hampshire's account, attach value to human individuality and singularity? One answer points to observable, by means of history or introspection, facts of human nature. The other, and more interesting and controversial answer, is that which seeks to supply reasons why we ought to value, cultivate and express individuality. In Hampshire's scheme, this is of crucial importance for his argument. The central role of the contrast that he makes between procedure and substance is tied to a defence of the proposition that there is a set of reasons that constitute arguments for the value of individuality that, with the value of procedural justice, are fundamental and invariant elements in all defensible conceptions of the good.

This is, of course, an impossible task if we think of political and moral theory in terms of offering strict proofs. One of the distinctive aspects of Hampshire's approach to political thought is his open recognition that in questions of this kind there is no way of proving in a rigorous sense that there is anything incoherent in not recognizing that procedural justice is a virtue of the kind he claims it to be. 'These are arguments only. There is no proof of this, or of any other, proposition in political philosophy.'[109] Nevertheless, it is possible to present the reasons why it is desirable to see morality as possessing these two interdependent aspects of the substantive and the procedural. The thin procedural concept of justice that Hampshire invokes is put forward as an antidote to the view that arguments between competing and different conceptions of the good must ultimately reach some end point where reason no longer applies. As far as Hampshire is concerned, this cannot be true either as a matter of historical fact or of logic.

The question that arises here is this: 'Can a thin, procedural concept of justice have an imaginative power in the minds of people, more powerful than the appeals to freedom, familiar in the rhetoric of nationalism and tribalism all over the world?'[110] This is a question that strikes at the heart of Hampshire's account and it is a question that is not easy to answer on purely philosophical grounds. One line of attack is to argue for congruence between the historical imagination and respect for procedural justice. Hampshire points out that arguments in negotiations often turn to a consideration of precedents and comparisons of similar cases that have to be understood within their own historical context. Support for this view is also found in the history of political thought, in Hume and Burke, for example. Both, if with different emphases, took the long-term survival of institutions throughout human history as a significant fact that ought not to be ignored. Furthermore, the sense of our embeddedness within traditions with a historical and cultural continuity ought to encourage a respect for and, indeed, an encouragement of their diversity.

Given the importance attached to the characteristics of context, it does not follow that the claims and duties that support procedural justice and fairness are completely untouched by particular conceptions of the good. Although the minimum form of justice that Hampshire is arguing for attempts to steer clear of claims to absoluteness, it is specific in its demand that the procedures of fair discussion, negotiation and compromise are recognized. Despite the fact that the human world is regarded as 'the intersecting histories of competing religions, competing languages and customs, competing cultures, competing conceptions of the good, competing systems of government', it is clear that:

> [no] games theory, no ingenious mechanisms of rational choice, can help in moral conflicts as they might with competing appetites and interests. No appeal to a possible unanimity and to a possible sentimental harmony, as in Rousseau, have proved to be plausible. No project of unanimity by conquest and take-over, as in Hegel and Marx, is either plausible or morally acceptable. No doctrine of universal human rights can convincingly be represented as independent of a particular, historically traceable conception of the good and of the freedom of the individual as a primary good.

At the same time, Hampshire argues, this plurality of values itself produces an 'unavoidable and trans-historical predicament', whereby we are forced to discuss and negotiate within the framework of just procedures.[111]

Hampshire's discussion of moral conflict is especially interesting because it is explicitly bound up with reflection on the
nature of history, politics and the limitations of our knowledge
in these domains. Hampshire's meditation upon modern political disasters, especially those of the twentieth century, often
drawing upon his own direct experience, takes a direction that
runs counter to much contemporary political theorizing. The
stress upon the persistence of conflict in human affairs has a
particular relevance to the problem of the conflicting demands
of public and private morality. In contrast with much contemporary political theory, Hampshire is sceptical about the relevance or validity of the search for an account of an ideal
society or of essential human virtues. The truth that Hobbes
perceived is that 'the proper business of politics' is not to seek
the universal principles of justice but 'protection against the
perennial evils of human life – physical suffering, the destruc-
tions and mutilations of war, poverty and starvation, enslave-
ment and humiliation'.[112] Proposals for general principles of
social justice always seem 'to be trapped in circularity'.
Conclusions derived from their own arguments supply the only
criteria of rationality and acceptability that they are prepared
to accept. Hampshire has come, he says, to appreciate fully
Hume's statement that 'Reason both is, and ought to be, the
slave of the passions'. He translates this into the more modern
idiom of political philosophy as: 'In moral and political philosophy one is looking for adequate premises from which to infer
conclusions already and independently accepted because of
one's feelings and sympathies.'[113]

Here, again, the contrast between substance and procedure
that is central for Hampshire's account comes into play. His
response is framed in terms of the basic contrast that he draws
between substantive and procedural values. Hampshire's argument is that if we recognize this distinction, then we can accept
that, although there may be many different conceptions of the
good, this does not prevent us from seeing that some of them
are indefensible. They can be challenged in terms of those
errors of fact or of logic they commit that undermine the
reasons they give for their acceptance. Further, there is nothing
to prevent us from saying that some conceptions of the good
are downright evil. The downright evil nature of some conceptions of the good can be affirmed on the basis, at the least, of

their lack of respect for the minimalist concept of trans-historical procedural justice that Hampshire wants to defend. In contrast to the diversity of and conflict between rival conceptions of the good, Hampshire contends that we can indicate 'a minimum of decent fairness' that is a value independent of any conception of the good.

This distinction between substantive and procedural values opens the way to a response to the problem posed by Machiavelli's political thought. In short, Hampshire's response, which is similar to Berlin's, is to assert that we can recognize the existence of 'a recognizable basic level of common human decency' connected to the notion of a minimum procedural justice. However, Hampshire is clear that his recognition of the power of argument present in 'common everyday rationality' is a weak form of protection against those constant and undeniable evils such as massacre, starvation, imprisonment, torture, death and mutilation in war, tyranny and humiliation'. This is a deeply pessimistic conclusion.[114]

The problem of the crucial role that the distinction between form and substance plays here emerges very clearly in Joshua Cohen's response to Hampshire's criticism of his and Rawls's political liberalism.[115] Cohen rightly points out that both political liberals, such as himself, and Hampshire accept the reality and the challenge of moral pluralism in modern democratic states. However, he argues that political liberalism does not see the need to accept Hampshire's pessimistic response to the problem of pluralism. This is especially so, according to Cohen, because there is a basic weakness in Hampshire's position. This, he argues, derives from the role that the distinction between substance and procedure plays in Hampshire's argument. Cohen argues that there appears to be a clear contradiction in Hampshire's account of both the need for and the possibility of agreement over fair procedures when combined with a scepticism and alarm over the need for agreement over substantive principles, such as competing conceptions of justice.

Cohen characterizes Hampshire's position as a version of 'democratic pluralism'. The 'democratic pluralist', Cohen perceives, is committed to a view that drives a wedge between substantive and procedural values. As he puts it, 'in a nutshell', democratic pluralism as advocated by Hampshire argues that 'moral pluralism is compatible with agreement on rules of a democratic political game, but not with more substantive agreement'.

The most important of Hampshire's claims that Cohen rejects is that the disagreements moral pluralism inevitably generates about non-procedural issues of social justice mean that the hope for agreement on a substantive conception is unrealistic and utopian. Cohen argues that Hampshire's view of the impact of pluralism is, in fact, a familiar one in American political and constitutional thought. Conceptions of constitutional design and democratic theory advanced in the work of Holmes, Ely, Ackerman, Harold Laski and Robert Dahl belong in this tradition. Using Rawlsian language, he states that:

> democratic pluralism endorses (as consistent with moral pluralism) the idea of constitutional consensus – an agreement on the 'political procedures of democratic government'. But it rejects the possibility that Rawls holds out – of a deeper and broader overlapping consensus. A consensus is broader if it extends beyond political procedures and the rights required for them, to matters of liberty of conscience and freedom of thought, fair equality of opportunity, and fair distribution; it is deeper if it reaches conceptions of the person and such abstract values as fairness, rather than simply rules and principles. Democratic pluralism, then, rejects depth and breadth not as intrinsically unattractive, but as incompatible with moral pluralism.[116]

Cohen's strategy, endorsed by Rawls, is to challenge the relevance of the distinction between procedure and substance that is central for Hampshire's argument. Upholding this distinction is, as we have seen, essential for Hampshire's idea of the nature and scope of political theory. Cohen describes his own position as 'democratic-egalitarian'. This is in contrast not only with Hampshire's 'democratic pluralism' but also with two other views. These are ascribed to the 'nihilist' and the 'communitarian'. The nihilist argues that as procedure and substance are subject to the same constraints, moral pluralism undermines the prospects of agreement in both. The communitarian agrees that substance and procedure are subject to the same limitations, but tries to limit the threat of pluralism either by denying it as an important fact or by arguing for moral agreement as an ideal. In putting forward this classification of responses to pluralism, Cohen wants to highlight the fact that

Hampshire's account stands out in that it is distinctive, among these four standpoints, in arguing that moral pluralism 'drives a wedge between procedural and substantive views'.[117]

Cohen's main line of argument against Hampshire is to claim that the basic weakness in his position lies in the mistake of thinking of democracy in purely formal or procedural terms. In contrast, democracy must be understood as both a procedural and a substantive ideal. Procedure and substance stand on an equal footing in democratic thought. If Hampshire can argue that the reality of moral pluralism can be consistent with the attainment of procedural agreement, then, Cohen argues, there is no reason why consensus cannot also be achieved on substantive issues or, to put it more accurately in Rawlsian terms, the construction of an overlapping consensus over a political conception of justice. The argument turns on the claim that, as Hampshire is unable to convincingly drive a wedge between procedural and substantive aspects of democracy, he is unsuccessful in his attempt to deny the possibility of achieving a consensus, if only an 'overlapping' one.

What is at stake here, in the contrast between the views of political liberals such as Cohen and Rawls and Hampshire, is a fundamental difference of perception. Hampshire refers to his own standpoint as 'a metaphysical vision, a speculation'. In advancing this 'speculation', Hampshire draws upon several sources from the history of moral and political thought for inspiration. Hume supplies the insight that our opinions about substantive justice arise from natural human sentiments filtered through the variable circumstances of history and custom. Hume, however, also believed that the existence of a constant human nature would set limits to our sentiments in the direction of harmony and agreement. Furthermore, the 'metaphysical vision' to which Hampshire refers gains its inspiration from Spinoza. He derives from Spinoza the principle that 'diversity, rather than conformity, is not a moral prescription' but a 'natural necessity'.[118]

Hampshire's response to Cohen and other similar arguments is simply to argue that they overstate the possibility and the necessity for substantive agreement. The claim that Hampshire is 'driving a wedge' between procedure and substance is not the most helpful way of describing his argument. For example, it is not at all clear that Cohen's description of democracy applies with equal force to Hampshire's idea of a minimalist proceduralism. It is clearly inaccurate to say that Hampshire's account of procedural justice is a wholly consensual affair. As far as Hampshire is concerned, every 'appeal to precedent in a political procedural dispute, and every appeal to equality of access, is open to dispute' and 'disputes about the just and fair political procedures and institutions will continue indefinitely'.[119]

4 John Gray: Pluralism and Modus Vivendi

The tension between a pessimistic and a more benign version of pluralism emerges in a stark form in the work of John Gray. The starting point for an appreciation of this aspect of Gray's political thought is to be found in his interpretation of Isaiah Berlin's concept of value pluralism. In Gray's view, Berlin was an intellectual hedgehog, whose thought was animated by a central idea of 'enormous subversive force'.[120] This is, of course, the idea of value pluralism. Gray, however, explicates and emphasizes the agonistic, existential and tragic interpretation of Berlin's pluralism.

John Gray's account of the implications of value pluralism must be placed within the context of his progressive disenchantment with mainstream Anglo-American political theory and with western civilization itself. Notably, he has objected to the excessive narrowness and artificiality of much of the academically respectable version of political theory that is generally taught in western universities. Much of what Gray has had to say about the state of academic political theory has found a sympathetic audience. However, this sympathy has probably been tested to an extreme degree by some of Gray's recent philosophical excursions.[121] There is a concern, however, with three interrelated themes that seem to mark out the main direction of Gray's most recent work in political theory. These are the rejection of those aspects of modernity that are presumed to be the consequence of an 'Enlightenment project' – the idea that value pluralism presents a central problem for political theory, and the response to the challenge that both of these are thought to present. The result is an argument for the theory and practice of 'modus vivendi'.

Gray's account of value pluralism can be placed within a tradition of European disenchantment with the Enlightenment that is as old as the Enlightenment itself. This form of anti-Enlightenment thought is powerfully represented in the thought of Nietzsche and Heidegger, both of whom are referred to approvingly by Gray.[122] In addition, and in a way that has become commonplace but is still no less controversial, Gray talks repeatedly of an 'Enlightenment project'. Such language is often criticized by specialists concerned with the history of the Enlightenment. As far as they are concerned, it seems that the more they examine it the more complex our picture of the Enlightenment becomes, even to the extent that the term might itself become obscure or meaningless. In fact, it appears that the existence of a coherent Enlightenment project seems to be most obvious for those who want to reject it, while those who examine it most closely are more likely to find its supposed unity dissolving into a mass of particulars.[123] Nevertheless, Gray could argue that the question of historical accuracy is irrelevant to the general argument that he is making. If this is so, then what seems to be going on here is that the idea of the existence of an 'Enlightenment project' is being used more as a projection that attempts to give historical and intellectual legitimacy to contemporary political commitments, rather than as a statement claiming historical or philosophical accuracy.[124]

Gray's advocacy of the idea of value pluralism owes much to his critical engagement with the work of Isaiah Berlin. However, the precise nature of the relationship between the first theme, of hostility to the Enlightenment, and the second theme, of value pluralism, is not altogether clear. Although it can be argued that they are conceptually distinct theses, it is certainly true that in the case of many who have made similar points there is no doubt concerning the effect each has on the other. The third major theme in Gray's recent work is the presentation of a theory of modus vivendi as the best way to maintain what is valuable and philosophically defensible from the ruins of modern liberalism.

Gray's most recent work is animated by an almost total rejection of western modernity and its supposed foundations in an 'Enlightenment project'. According to Gray's diagnosis, western civilization is best understood as a self-destructive

nihilistic project. Despite this thoroughgoing negative diagnosis, however, Gray also wants to argue the case for a form of
political life that he calls 'agonistic' or 'modus vivendi' liberalism, or 'post-liberalism'. This seems puzzling. If western civilization, whether the product of an 'Enlightenment project' or
not, is so doomed, then why bother to defend any form of
liberalism, modus vivendi or any other, at all?

In Gray's words, the political message of 'the Enlightenment
project' (if we accept for the moment that there ever was such
a thing) is in a state of 'world-historical collapse'.[125] Gray clearly
endorses the view, itself a mark of the counter-Enlightenment,
that the Enlightenment must be thought of as a self-conscious
project designed and carried out by a relatively small group of
early modern philosophers.[126] Curiously, Gray's constant appeal
to the idea of an 'Enlightenment project' can itself be regarded
as a symptom of modernity. Gray paints with a broad brush
when he discusses the Enlightenment and the counter-Enlightenment. As a consequence, there is a general lack of detail in
his arguments and some fairly controversial, and generally
unsubstantiated, claims are made.[127]

An important move in Gray's progressive disenchantment
with the dominant schools of Anglo-American political theory
can be found in his interpretation of and enthusiasm for the
work of Isaiah Berlin. Gray is inspired by the idea of value
pluralism in Berlin's work. Gray's own proposal of a theory of
'agonistic liberalism' owes much to Berlin's influence. This,
however, has itself evolved into a theory of 'post-liberal pluralism' that seems to be at odds with the general direction of
Berlin's political thought. This particular construction, in turn,
proposes that the most realistic response to the disenchanted
and post-liberal predicament is to embrace a form of pluralism
that Berlin would probably have found uncongenial.

In Gray's opinion, the true implication of Berlin's political
thought must reside in the acceptance of a radical value pluralism that has the unintended consequence of undermining the
claims of traditional liberalism. The outcome of this diagnosis
is an argument for a form of what Gray calls 'agonistic liberalism'. The key question then becomes one of its coherence and
viability. While many of the tensions in Berlin's political
thought rest upon the way in which he was influenced by the
divergent calls of both his favourite Enlightenment thinkers

and their Romantic critics, Gray's argument is far more (one-sidedly) indebted to the ideas of the counter-Enlightenment. The campaign that he is fighting is much more unambiguously an assault upon the Enlightenment citadel. If this is so, then it is hard, ultimately, to accept the use to which the authority of Berlin is used in its support.

One of the most significant differences between Gray's and Berlin's pluralism is to be found in their interpretation of the nature of modernity. For Gray, this is tied in to his depiction and rejection of 'the Enlightenment project'. In his turn towards a 'modus vivendi' response to modern pluralism, Gray also draws inspiration from Hobbes. What seems to ensue is an unstable mixture, drawing upon the seemingly incompatible influences of Berlin, Hobbes and Oakeshott. Gray often refers to the influence of Michael Oakeshott, one of the most significant of Hobbes's interpreters, although its precise nature is not easy to decipher. One aspect of this is clear. Gray has referred to both Berlin and Oakeshott as important thinkers who have upheld a style of political thought that stands in stark contrast to the predominant forms of modern academic liberal theorizing. In addition, the political thought of both Berlin and Oakeshott is commended for avoiding a reliance upon ideas of consensus and rational choice.[128]

In response to what he considers to be the central Anglo-American orthodoxy, Gray offers a 'neo-Hobbesian philosophy of modus vivendi' as his response to the condition of modern pluralism. But, of course, just as Berlin's theory of value pluralism need not necessarily lend support for liberalism, as Gray has himself argued, it is equally true that Hobbes's philosophy does not provide unambiguously clear support for Gray's agonistic alternative either. After all, as has been pointed out many times, Hobbes did not believe that a stable peace within or between states could be based upon a modus vivendi. The whole idea of the 'generation of the Sovereign' in 'Leviathan' is to enable us to escape from the uncertainty of this state of affairs. And one might also add that, as far as Hobbes was concerned, this arena of civil life can never escape completely from 'the natural condition' of war in contrast to the prospect of cultural coexistence that Gray at times refers to.[129] Nevertheless, Gray characterizes his response to the challenge of modern pluralism as a form of 'neo-Hobbesian liberalism'.

Labels are not the most important things in political theory, but this self-characterization ought to put us on guard against other contestable interpretations or 'creative misreadings' in Gray's account.

The precise nature of the relationship between Berlin's pluralism and his liberalism is still a controversial topic. John Gray's interpretation of Berlin's political thought has the merit of bringing into the open many of its inherent tensions and problems. His central argument is that 'Berlin's master-thesis of value pluralism, which is defined as a thesis of the incommensurability, or incomparability by reason, of rivalrous goods and evils and forms of life, has the role in his thought of privileging choice-making as the embodiment of human self-creation'.[130] However, Gray's interpretation of Berlin's pluralism emphasizes what he sees as the more existentialist and 'decisionist' aspects of his thought. At the same time, he joins the ranks of a small but controversial band of political thinkers who question the way in which Berlin and some pluralists seem to accept the idea of coherence between pluralism and liberalism.

According to Gray, there are three main ways in which Berlin connects pluralism to liberalism. The first rests upon Berlin's defence of the value of negative liberty. If the quality of 'self-creation' is emphasized, then, on Gray's account, negative liberty is the pre-eminent value because 'it facilitates human self-creation by choice-making among goods and evils that are rationally incomparable. Value-pluralism supports liberalism here in that it is by the choices protected by negative freedom that we negotiate our way among incommensurable values.'[131] The second component of Gray's interpretation of Berlin's attempt to link pluralism and liberalism rests on the argument that, as values are rationally incommensurable, it must follow that no state or other political authority can have good reason to impose any particular values or combination of values upon its citizens. If values are plural, then it can also be argued, as does Bernard Williams, that the consciousness of this pluralism is itself a good.[132] It is a mark of authoritarian or illiberal regimes, in contrast, to deny the truth of pluralism.

Gray sees Berlin as the author of a highly distinctive form of liberalism. He goes so far as to say that Berlin's liberalism is 'the most profoundly deliberated, and most powerfully defended, in our time, or, perhaps, in any time'.[133] In saying this, as Michael Walzer pointed out, Gray was inadvertently assuming that Berlin's liberalism is itself not incommensurable with other twentieth-century forms of liberalism.[134] However, even if that is right, Gray claims that the distinctive character of Berlin's liberalism resides in what he calls its 'agonistic' character. Gray's interpretation of the significance of Berlin's work is stated in highly dramatic and portentious terms. The idea of pluralism that 'animates all of Berlin's work, both in intellectual history and in political theory, is one which, if true, as I take it to be, strikes a death-blow to the central, classical Western tradition – and, it must be added, to the project of the Enlightenment'.[135] The 'agonistic' character of this new form of liberalism resides in the fact that:

> ultimate values are objective and knowable, but they are many, they often come into conflict with one another and are uncombinable in a single human being or a single society, and that in many of such conflicts there is no overarching standard whereby the competing claims of such ultimate values are rationally arbitrable. Conflicts among such values are conflicts among incommensurables, and the choices we make among them are bound to be radical and, often, tragic choices. There is, then, no *summum bonum* or *logos*, no Aristotelian mean or Platonic form of the good, no perfect form of human life, which we may never find but towards which we may struggle, no measuring rod on which different forms of human life encompassing different and uncombinable goods can be ranked. This assertion of the variety and incommensurability of the goods of human life is not, it is worth noting, the Augustinian thesis that human life is imperfect, and imperfectible: it is the thesis that the very idea of perfection is incoherent.[136]

This means that Berlin, in putting forward a new agonistic form of liberalism, recognizes a thoroughgoing pluralism of values that includes the negative and positive liberties, and is arguing for something that is clearly distinct from the main forms of contemporary liberal theory with its obsessive concern to discover reasonably acceptable foundations for theories of rights and justice. Indeed, the radical nature of Gray's interpretation of the true implications of Berlin's pluralism is shown in his claim that it produces not only a distinct form of liberalism, but, more significantly, that it undercuts all rival forms. The reason given for this is simply that if value pluralism is true, then liberty can only be one of many other incommensurable values. Berlin's own famous working of the distinction between positive and negative liberty itself illustrates, it is claimed, the reality of the incommensurability and conflict between rival values.

Gray's conclusion is that the lesson to be learnt from this is that if we accept the truth of value pluralism we must acknowledge the limits of rationality and embrace the fact of radical choice between incommensurable values. Gray softens his argument a little when he concedes that where there is a conflict of values a way for resolving such a conflict will, often, be suggested by the cultural context. This is, perhaps, where an Oakeshottian remedy is being offered for a Berlinian problem. However, this is in stark contrast to Berlin's suggestion that when possible we ought to look for trade-offs and compromise between conflicting values and goods, even when we know that there is no principle that shows it to be the most rational solution. In facing up to this problem, Berlin agreed that, in the context of 'the fallacy of realizing ultimate harmony', the problem of the existence of mutually exclusive choices as the foundation of human creativity seems to have no clear answer.

Berlin, however, went one step further in not leaving the argument there. As far as he was concerned, there was an obligation to 'soften' those unavoidable collisions of values. At the heart of Berlin's political thought there is a tension between the emphasis upon the reality of pluralism and the recognition of the danger of dramatizing the incompatibility of values. There seem to be two motivating ideas at the heart of Berlin's support for the idea of pluralism. Pluralism is enlisted as an intellectual weapon against the appeal of perfection that, for Berlin, writing in post-war Europe, means Nazi and especially Soviet totalitarianism. On this, there can be no compromise. On the other hand, non-totalitarian states can aim for an 'uneasy equilibrium' that is the 'necessary precondition for decent societies and morally acceptable behaviour'. Berlin wanted, ultimately, to enlist his controversial thesis of value pluralism in defence of the principles of the Enlightenment. In Gray's case, the fact and the theory of value pluralism undermine it.

One of the most controversial claims to emerge from Gray's interpretation of Berlin's work is that if we accept the full implications of the truth of pluralism, then we are led to the inescapable conclusion that liberal regimes cannot claim to have a privileged position. In Gray's words, where:

> liberal values come into conflict with others which depend for their existence on non-liberal social or political structures and forms of life, and where these values are truly incommensurables, there can – if pluralism is true – be no argument according universal priority to liberal values. To deny this is to deny the thesis of the incommensurability of values.[137]

It is this claim that separates Gray's argument from what he refers to as 'the weak form of pluralism'. The mistake made by weak pluralists, according to Gray, is that, although they accept the uncombinability of values or human goods, they maintain that they are open to rational comparability. Controversially, Gray avoids this option. He gives two reasons. He asserts that this is clearly not Berlin's position. Even more controversially, he asserts that claims that comparability is compatible with incommensurability would require a general theory or general account, such as that provided by classical utilitarianism, to deliver a framework for rational choice. This is clearly a highly controversial view where the weight of argument is not conclusive. Although Gray admits that reasoning about value conflicts is possible within particular contexts, it does not follow, as he implies, that we ought to think any universal principles have to be involved. The main point Gray derives from this suggestion is that given that we accept the reality of value pluralism as he describes it, then liberal values, that is, the values embodied in liberal institutions, are unable to claim any privileged status. Liberal ways of life cannot claim any kind of uncontested superiority over non-liberal ways of life. As a consequence, Gray claims that the true message of Berlin's liberal pluralism is the creation of a form of 'agonistic liberalism' that is clearly distinct from all other traditional forms of liberalism.

In short, it appears that Gray's portrayal of Berlin as 'the Nietzsche of All Souls' indicates but also exaggerates some of the apparent uncertainties to be found in his thought.[138] More

to the point, it also shows how the idea of value pluralism can
be fused with other notions that owe more to the general
permeation of postmodernist and counter-Enlightenment
ideas than they do to traditional liberalism. Nevertheless,
Gray's work is instructive and challenging. Although he claims
a Berlinian inspiration when taking on these issues, there is
one area where Gray is clearly un-Berlinian. This is his general
attitude to the Enlightenment. The key move in Gray's
transition from his earlier liberalism to his later 'post-liberal'
and pluralist standpoint would appear to be the relatively
undertheorized endorsement of a theory of radical pluralism.
However, the addition of an outright condemnation of the
'Enlightenment project' and of the 'nihilism' inherent in
western civilization provides the guiding thread to Gray's
reflections. The thesis of radical value pluralism combined with
a general hostility to the ideas held to constitute the core of
the 'Enlightenment project' provide support for each other.
But, if this is so, one is still left wondering why this move does
not deepen the nihilism of modernity. Is it possible to have a
viable form of liberalism that so resolutely rejects the ideals of
the Enlightenment as they are generally understood, irrespec-
tive of whether they can be correctly thought of as emanating
from a 'project'? Gray's answer comes in the form of a third
kind of liberalism that attempts to do without the support of
Enlightenment ideas.

Gray sees the only viable future for liberalism as a form of
modus vivendi. He argues that liberalism has two faces; it
contains two contrasting philosophies:

> In one, toleration is justified as a means to truth. In this view,
> toleration is an instrument of rational consensus, and a diversity
> of ways of life is endured in the faith that it is destined to dis-
> appear. In the other, toleration is valued as a condition of peace,
> and divergent ways of living are welcomed as marks of diversity
> in the good life. The first conception supports an ideal of ulti-
> mate convergence on values, the latter an ideal of *modus
> vivendi*.[139]

For Gray, liberalism must abandon any idea of achieving a
rational consensus and must seek, instead, a modus vivendi as
its basic rationale. Gray also describes this as a move back from

Kant to Hobbes as the best source of inspiration for political thought under modern conditions.

Clearly, the first version owes much to Kant and Rawls, while the second is derived primarily from a controversial interpretation of Hobbes. Gray also mentions in this context both Isaiah Berlin and Michael Oakeshott as exemplars of this more restrained form of liberalism. It would seem that at the heart of Gray's thought here we can detect an unstable mixture of an Oakeshott-inspired rejection of all forms of rationalism in politics and a Berlin-inspired espousal of the truth of pluralism. Where Gray, it must be presumed, departs from the the spirit of Berlin's political thought must reside in his fundamental idea that value pluralism undermines the claims of liberalism.

Of course, it can be argued that Gray is pointing to a dilemma that has been noted many times in Berlin's pluralism. This is to the effect that a radical pluralism that stresses the radical incommensurability of values does not, in itself, establish the primacy of liberalism or of liberal values. Berlin's pluralism, if taken to its logical conclusion, the argument goes, undermines his liberalism. In fact, it is argued, Berlin's support for liberalism is derived from considerations other than his avowed pluralism.[140]

In contrast to Berlin, Gray's expressed aim, despite his apocalyptic warnings about civilizational doom, is to argue for a form of modus vivendi liberalism. Gray presents himself as an opponent of all forms of foundationalism in political theory. However, it is clear that his version of value pluralism, which is itself best understood as a highly controversial theory, plays a foundational role in his account of modus vivendi. '*Modus vivendi* articulates a view of the good. It is an application of value pluralism to political practice.' Given his characterization of liberalism as having two faces, Gray is forced to place all liberal political thinkers into either one of these two categories. This is one place where the trouble begins. Although Gray's dichotomy is extremely useful, the problem in forcing a complex tradition into this categorial dichotomy is that it is bound to lead to serious misrepresentation of the main rival theories, as well as of his own. The question is whether the operation of modus vivendi can provide a 'renewal of the liberal project' that is genuinely distinctive and superior to its rivals.[141]

The obvious rival theory here is the political liberalism championed most notably by John Rawls. The problem then arising is that Rawls's theory of political liberalism has been created on the basis of an attempt to answer some of the same problems as Gray's modus vivendi. However, Rawls's 'anti-philosophical' and 'anti-universalist' theory does not fit easily into Gray's dichotomy. If this is so, then there must be room for at least one other face of liberalism.[142] It is misleading to dismiss Rawls's theory, as Gray does, as being just another form of Enlightenment liberalism. Rawls's discussion and rejection of the claims made for modus vivendi play a central role in his argument for political liberalism. Rawls, it must be remembered, rejected the idea of a modus vivendi on the grounds that it would be inherently unstable. Gray has not demonstrated that Rawls's alternative of an 'overlapping consensus' is unworkable. Whatever our verdict might be on the success of Rawls's political liberalism, it is clear that his idea of public reason and of an overlapping consensus is meant to be a 'post-Enlightenment' alternative to the two versions of liberalism that Gray offers.

Gray's own solution of modus vivendi either promises too much or too little. In effect, Gray smuggles in through the back door the considerations that he found so objectionable in other forms of liberalism, including those clearly belonging to the Enlightenment tradition. According to Gray:

> Liberals and pluralists walk side by side in resisting totalitarian and fundamentalist regimes. *Modus vivendi* is impossible in a regime in which the varieties of the good are seen as symptoms of error or heresy. Without institutions in which different ways of life are accorded respect there cannot be peaceful coexistence between them. Where liberal regimes foster this coexistence, pluralists are bound to support them.[143]

This clearly claims much more for a modus vivendi than we were initially led to expect. Here Gray is making the value of respect for other ways of life central for the stability of his version of modus vivendi. He is also assuming that rational citizens of a regime of modus vivendi would prefer compromise to conflict. It is hard to see in this where the clear difference exists between Gray's modus vivendi and some of the versions of liberalism that he wants to reject. The problem is that Gray's modus vivendi alternative to the nihilism engendered by the 'Enlightenment project' itself relies upon the assumption that citizens of a post-liberal state have accepted the truth of value pluralism. But value pluralism is itself a highly controversial theory and, as such, it is hard to see how it could provide support for a political regime. In other words, Gray's solution to the problem of pluralism does not escape from the difficulties that he identified in Enlightenment liberalism. His own account of modus vivendi rests upon the general acceptance of the controversial comprehensive doctrine of value pluralism (to use Rawlsian terminology). It would appear that the kinds of people who would inhabit Gray's modus vivendi society would have to be the kind of people that many Enlightenment thinkers hoped would be the citizens of the future; tolerant citizens of a liberal state.[144] Furthermore, insofar as there are to be limits to what can count as a legitimate form of modus vivendi, it seems that Gray has not escaped making the kind of universalist claims that he has otherwise condemned. The problem is that we cannot both totally dispense with the ideas that we owe to the Enlightenment and argue for any form of liberal regime, even if it takes the form of a 'modus vivendi'.

Conclusion

Much of modern political thought since Weber has to a large degree been held captive by a set of images of decline and of loss. Ideas that the modern age is in 'a period of decline, a loss of values, a forgetfulness of being and a general disenchantment' ought not, perhaps, to be accepted so uncritically as they have been.[145] They are as contestable as any other political ideas. Although the question of the pluralism of values is one that seems to be unavoidable, it is not clear that it has to be necessarily linked to the idea of a historical development of disenchantment as Weber and others describe it. Nevertheless, it does seem that most contemporary political thought does work with the idea associated with Weber that there is something peculiarly modern about pluralism and that it is linked to disenchantment. Larmore, in a statement that is representative of this mood, has stressed that 'pluralism is indeed a distinctively modern doctrine. It belongs to a disenchanted vision of the world, which sees itself as having abandoned the comfort of finding in the harmony of the cosmos or in God's providential ordering of the world the one ultimate source of value.'[146]

It is not too surprising given this intellectual background that political thinkers such as Weber, Berlin, Hampshire and Gray have drawn pessimistic conclusions from their engagement with the problem of pluralism. Even when they make allowance for the practice of compromise, judgment, and the operation of practical reason they still find themselves unable to avoid the thought that recognition of the challenge of value pluralism must seriously transform our political understanding in a pessimistic direction even if only to remind us of the limitations of our political knowledge and practice.

3

Reconciliation and Public Reason

1 John Rawls: The Idea of a 'Realistic Utopia'

The problem of value pluralism and disagreement is a central concern that runs throughout John Rawls's work. In his first published article he asked whether a reasonable and rational decision procedure could be found for adjudicating between conflicting ideas and interests.[1] In his later writings Rawls argues that the most important task of contemporary political philosophy is to produce an adequate response to what he considers to be the undeniable fact that modern democratic societies are shaped by a plurality of opposed but 'reasonable comprehensive doctrines'. Rawls's concern with pluralism cannot be fully understood without placing it within the context of the basic intuitions and aims of his political thought. As Rawls has stated that all 'moral doctrines contain normative concepts and principles combined with elements of human psychology and political sociology, together with other institutional and historical assumptions', we are justified in reading his work in these same terms.[2] Putting it straightforwardly, Rawls describes the basic intention that informs his work as the construction of a public philosophy that would support the survival of a reasonably just constitutional democracy.[3] Behind this, there is a deeper set of worries. Of these, the thought that politics might be no more than 'simply the struggle for power and influence – everyone trying to get their own way' would be unbearable if true.[4] Working within a broadly conceived contractualist tradition, Rawls's response to these fears is to endorse a view of political philosophy, certainly within a pluralist society, as a public philosophy seeking to find the bases for agreement.

In a way that is similar to Berlin's interpretation of the history of moral and political philosophy, Rawls argues there is a deep division between the dominant tradition that holds there is one true conception of the good and an alternative tradition that recognizes the existence of a plurality of reasonable but opposing doctrines of the good.[5] The problem, more precisely, is that:

> modern democratic society is characterized not by a pluralism of comprehensive religious, philosophical, and moral doctrines but by a pluralism of incompatible but reasonable comprehensive doctrines. No one of these doctrines is affirmed by citizens generally. Nor should one expect that in the foreseeable future one of them, or some other reasonable doctrine, will ever be affirmed by all, or nearly all, citizens. The quest of the dominant tradition for a comprehensive doctrine that would be agreed upon by all reasonable citizens within a constitutional regime cannot succeed under condtions of modern pluralism. Political liberalism assumes that, for political purposes, a plurality of reasonable but incompatible doctrines is the normal result of the exercise of human reason within the framework of the free institutions of a constitutional democratic regime.[6]

The obvious question is to ask why the existence of a plurality of reasonable doctrines is such a problem. One reason is that the fact of pluralism creates a difficult challenge for many modern liberals for whom justification has become a central problem. Liberal theorists have generally insisted that justifications of the exercise of political power must be available and intelligible for all citizens. However, if pluralism, understood as the existence of conflicting but reasonable visions of the good, is itself a product of the liberal state, then this seems to limit the prospects for the emergence of a universally acceptable public philosophy. This gives rise to the paradox of liberal justification. Liberal political regimes seem to create a state of affairs that undermines their own requirements for legitimacy.[7] Rawls's work, especially in its later form, is the most significant attempt to solve a problem that is inherent in the structure of modern liberalism. The problem or dilemma is produced by the tension that exists between the theory and the practice of the liberal state. The practice of liberal politics is committed to the encouragement of pluralism. At the same time, liberal theorists are committed to the idea of the superiority of liberalism over all other normative theories. But this can only be done by making the kind of claims that, according to the official doctrine, they are prevented from making if they want to remain neutral. The fact of pluralism makes this dilemma acute.[8]

This concern with reasonable pluralism is often taken to mark a radical redirection away from the preoccupations of Rawls's earlier work. It is sometimes argued that there are important differences between Rawls's earlier and later works. Alternatively, it is argued that it is a mistake to regard them as being different versions of the same theory.[9] Although there are differences of strategy and structure between the early work, leading up to and including *A Theory of Justice*, and the rethinking of that work that culminated in *Political Liberalism*, as well as the restatement of the theory in *Justice as Fairness*, it is also clear that there is a concern with, at least, one basic problem that can be traced throughout his work. This is the problem of how to respond to the existence of plural and conflicting moral and political values. In his earliest published paper Rawls outlined the problem of developing a rational method for adjudicating between conflicting moral rules and the decisions based upon them.[10] There is a clear continuity between this question and the explicit concern of the later work with the political problem of pluralism.

Rawls argues that 'the aims of political philosophy depend upon the society it addresses'.[11] He sees his theory in all its various formulations as a response to the basic problems typically experienced by a modern liberal and democratic society. The fact that the society Rawls describes bears more than a passing resemblance to the contemporary United States, or, more accurately, to a particular image of that society, is not his primary concern. It is therefore not surprising that many of Rawls's critics argue that his 'ideal theory' of justice is 'a conception of a liberal-democratic political constitution that turns out to be an idealized version of existing American

constitutional arrangements'.[12] This is not to say that Rawls's
political theory might not apply to other states with similar
characteristics. If it were to be applied to other states, then the
most important of those characteristics, in Rawls's view, is 'the
fact of reasonable pluralism'.

However, it is in his later work that the problem of 'reasonable pluralism' has come into the foreground. Two important
conceptual innovations that Rawls introduced in his later work
are the ideas of 'public reason' and a 'realistic utopia'. These
two concepts are linked by the idea of reconciliation. Although
not often mentioned in discussions of his work, it is the hope
for reconciliation, as his later work makes clear, that plays a
central and directing role in Rawls's political thought and his
response to pluralism. In its response to pluralism, the constant
reference to an ideal of reconciliation provides a clue for an
understanding of the presuppositions that underpin Rawls's
idea of the nature and purpose of modern political philosophy.
What are the aims of political philosophy when it addresses a
society characterized by value pluralism? Does the fact of pluralism require a rethinking of the role of the political philosopher? These questions are central for an understanding of
Rawls's idea of the nature of political philosophy and the
response that it ought to offer to the reality of pluralism and
disagreement.

Political philosophy in the modern democratic and pluralist
state, in Rawls's view, is best understood as forming a part of
the public political culture. If this is so, how are we to understand the nature and authority of the claims that he is making
as a political philosopher working within this context? Rawls
argues that, although it might be true that many of the great
political philosophers of the past thought deeply about their
relationship to their audience, it is the emergence of modern
forms of pluralism that has changed or ought to change fundamentally the way in which we understand the nature of that
relationship. This is, of course, despite Rawls's aim to steer
clear of philosophical controversy, a highly controversial interpretation of both the nature of modern culture and society and
of the nature of political philosophy.

The concepts of the political domain and of public reason
are at the heart of Rawls's account of political liberalism.
Looking at Rawls's theory in this way also leads to another

even deeper question. What is the right way to understand the nature of the theory that Rawls has proposed? It is usually assumed that Rawls's work ought to be understood in terms of its contribution to and revival of a tradition of grand theorizing in political philosophy. In keeping with this interpretation, it is common to find that *A Theory of Justice* is often compared with such classical texts as Plato's *Republic* and Hobbes's *Leviathan*. The implicit assumption here is that they are examples of the same kind of theoretical text and that their authors were engaged in the same kind of activity. Rawls's work is often acclaimed for its demonstration that this particular mode of abstract theorizing about politics in the modern world is still possible and desirable.

Another way of making sense of Rawls's theory and an explanation of why the concept of public reason plays such a central role is to think of it in a different way. This alternative way of looking at Rawls's work is to see it as having a different and much narrower focus than is normally assumed. Insufficient attention is paid to the fact that Rawls understands his theory straightforwardly as the construction of a defence of 'the possibility of a just constitutional democratic regime'.[13] If we look at Rawls's work in the way that he himself suggests we ought to, then some possible misunderstandings might be avoided. If we do so, Rawls's theory appears in a more interesting light, although this is not to deny that some new difficulties emerge. Of course, this is to assume that we ought to accept the accuracy of Rawls's self-description.

Throughout its development, an important feature of Rawls's work is that it takes seriously the problem of how we are to understand the role of the political philosopher in a democratic and pluralist society. Although many earlier political philosophers such as Plato and Hobbes were concerned to situate themselves within the framework cast by their own theories, Rawls was the first to see that the recognition of the significance of value pluralism poses a distinct and novel challenge. A revision of some of our entrenched beliefs is required. Instead of thinking of Rawls as 'adopting the authority of philosophy or theory, as a kind of scientist addressing reality or his fellow experts', we ought to 'see him as adopting the position of a citizen of a democratic regime addressing his fellow citizens'.[14] The problem here is that our fellow citizens will not necessarily share the same conceptions of the good with each other or with the political philosopher. It ought not to be overlooked that Rawls has been consistent not only in stating this fact, but in stressing that it is 'in general, a good thing that individuals' conceptions of their good should differ in significant ways'.[15] If this idea is accepted, then the political philosopher faces a dilemma. If the theory he proposes becomes too abstract it is in danger of losing contact with the problem that it is supposedly responding to in the first place, while if it stays close to that problem it is in danger of becoming nothing more than just one more set of policy recommendations that have no superior claim to authority over any other set of recommendations.

Rawls describes his later work as focusing on the construction of a 'realistic utopia'. This is a puzzling and seemingly contradictory concept. Rawls argues that political philosophy is 'realistically utopian' when 'it extends what are ordinarily thought to be the limits of practicable political possibility and, in so doing, reconciles us to our political and social condition'.[16] Rousseau's Social Contract provides one source of inspiration for the idea of a realistic utopia. The tension between utopianism and realism is brought out in Rousseau's statement that he is concerned with 'men as they are' and 'the laws as they can be'.[17] The reference to Rousseau is not incidental. Rawls takes these lines from Rousseau as a guide to the essential mixture of realism and utopia that he thinks is required by modern political philosophy if it is to have any genuine sense and purpose. The utopian element has two basic components. The first is the belief that 'the great evils of human history – unjust war and oppression, religious persecution and the denial of liberty of conscience, starvation and poverty, not to mention genocide and mass murder – follow from political injustice, with its own cruelties and callousness'. The other guiding idea is that 'once the gravest forms of political injustice are eliminated' these evils will disappear. Furthermore, there is a hope, probably derived from the influence of Rousseau, that people who live within a framework of just institutions will continuously affirm those institutions. As a consequence, such institutions are more likely to persist. The assumption here is that human nature is essentially good and that good institutions will nurture this natural goodness. Rawls argues that if the idea of such institutions can be endorsed and supported, then there is no overwhelming reason why they could not be brought into existence. In this sense, the utopian idea is also considered as being realistically feasible. But the utopian aspect is still predominant because citizens are able to realize all their fundamental interests.[18] Needless to say, what Rawls is referring to are those institutions that satisfy any of the 'reasonable liberal political conceptions of justice' that his own theory endorses as reasonable and just.

A problem that Rawls has in mind in his explication of his realistic utopia is the paradoxical nature of the origins of and transition to a just society. Rousseau provides an interesting example of this problem in his account of the legislator or lawgiver. This figure is introduced as a *deus ex machina* in his Social Contract, with the task of solving the problem of how 'the social spirit, which should be the result of the institution, would have to preside over the founding of the institution itself; and men would have to be prior to laws what they ought to become by means of laws'. Rawls, in his discussion of this idea, sees it less as a troubling paradox and more as a version of the traditional problem of order or stability. He defines the question in terms of the attempt to discover how institutions can generate the 'social spirit' that is presupposed and required by their need to be both enduring and stable.[19]

Rawls's description of his theory as a realistic utopia invites further reflection upon the inner structure of his political thought. Political philosophy, it can be argued, has both a persuasive and an ideal character. It 'presents an ideal of collective life, and it tries to show people one by one that they should live under it' .The problem is that these two ambitions may contradict each other and it may be impossible for them to be realized together. The problem is that 'an ideal, however attractive it may be to contemplate, is utopian if reasonable individuals cannot be motivated to live by it. But a political system that is completely tied down to individual motives may fail to embody any ideal at all.'[20] This problem of utopianism runs throughout Rawls's account of political liberalism. Nagel's description of this dilemma indicates some possible strategies that could be pursued in response. For example, the persuasive function of political theory could be subordinated to its ideal function. The argument would then be that if we can show that 'a certain form of political organization is the right one, that should be all the reason anyone needs to want it to be realized'. However, if 'real people find it psychologically very difficult or even impossible to live as the theory requires, or to adopt the relevant institutions, that should carry some weight against the ideal'.[21]

This way of describing the nature of political theory may sound unduly pessimistic. It is certainly true to say, as does Nagel, that these two functions of political philosophy fit together uneasily. Furthermore, and more radically, we may be led to doubt, on the basis of these considerations, whether the aims of political philosophy conceived in this way are ever achievable. The 'fact of reasonable pluralism' is bound to reinforce these doubts. If the task is to persuade individuals to accept principles that will motivate and command respect, then pluralism and the persistence of deep disagreement will make this task presumably even more difficult.

In addition to the problem of utopianism, Rawls has been criticized for constructing an excessively abstract theory. Not only is it too abstract, it is argued, it is also too far removed from political reality. Philosophy does not become political simply by treating political topics in a philosophical way; it must show some evidence of engagement with the political world.[22] Nevertheless, this criticism is not entirely fair to Rawls. He responds, in effect, by pointing out that the necessary abstraction of all political philosophy is 'set in motion by deep political conflicts'.[23] Indeed, in a way that resembles Berlin's account of the continuity and persistence of political philosophy, Rawls is clear that more often than not abstract theorizing is occasioned by the breakdown of shared political understanding.[24] It is far from Rawls's intention that political philosophy must withdraw from the world. Indeed, how could it? However, in contrast to Berlin, Weber and others, who share a more pessimistic and sceptical view of the implications of pluralism, it is Rawls's search for agreement and reconciliation that gives meaning and purpose to his theorizing. The hope here is that theorizing at a higher level of abstraction could provide an antidote to the continuous political disagreement that can be the consequence of plural and conflicting values. With this in mind, Rawls argues that it is most likely that 'the deeper the conflict, the higher the level of abstraction'.[25]

Although Rawls is concerned to stress the centrality of the fact of pluralism, he does not, at first sight, always seem to welcome it enthusiastically. Indeed, he makes it clear that it is not easy, in his opinion, to always accept the existence of 'profound and irreconcilable differences' in the 'reasonable comprehensive religious and philosophical conceptions of the world' of citizens. Nevertheless, the emergence of pluralism, on closer inspection, is more than just one historical possibility among others. It plays a providential role in Rawls's account of the tasks of reason. Pluralism has provided us with an important 'opportunity for the exercise of the highest moral powers'.[26]

The role of political philosophy in a pluralist world is to reconcile us to this fact by showing us 'the reason and indeed the political good and benefits of it'. Interestingly, Rawls admits there is the danger that a political philosophy such as his own theory of justice as fairness could be used ideologically in the Marxist sense of advancing a defence of an unworthy status quo.[27] It might be conscripted to play the role of a Platonic noble lie. Rawls's suggestion that political philosophy can be and ought to be 'realistically utopian' is meant to counter this suggestion. This is an extension of his idea of reconciliation. It probes 'the limits of practicable political possibility'. It is in this sense that Rawls thinks of political philosophy as being 'realistically utopian'. 'Our hope for the future of our society', he argues, 'rests on the belief that the social world allows at least a decent political order, so that a reasonably just, though not perfect democratic regime is possible.'[28] Clearly, Rawls's view of a realistically utopian theory, one that asks us what is politically possible under the conditions of a modern democratic society, cannot avoid consideration of the fact of pluralism. The aim is to reconcile us to this condition by showing us that it is a fact that we ought not to regret despite the problems and difficulties that it can produce.

A central feature of the rhetorical structure of Rawls's later work is its reliance upon what are claimed to be 'general facts of political sociology and human psychology'.[29] These 'facts' are clearly not 'brute facts', but are more like interpretations derived from or advanced in order to support his theory. Rawls is explicit about the function of these purported facts. He argues that any political theory or conception must have a view of the nature of the political and social world and derive an understanding of the existence and importance of such facts from that understanding. These 'facts' are meant to be well established and as uncontroversial as possible.

Rawls mentions five facts of this kind that are of central importance for his own theory. Four of them are the following: the fact of reasonable pluralism; the fact that shared adherence to one 'comprehensive doctrine' can be maintained only by the oppressive use of state power; a secure democratic regime must be freely supported by a majority of its politically active citizens; and that the political culture of a democratic society 'that has worked reasonably well' contains certain fundamental ideas from which it is possible to construct a suitable political conception of justice. These four facts are critically dependent upon the fifth fact, the burdens of judgement. The burdens of judgement are the source of disagreement. The basic idea is that reasonable disagreement is to be expected from such facts as the problem of assessing and evaluating the evidence, disagreement about the weight of relevant factors, the vagueness of concepts and the need for interpretation in hard cases, the inevitable differences in experience within modern societies, and the general complexity of the relevant normative considerations. Rawls sums this all up by saying that when we consider many of our most important political judgements that involve our basic political values, it is highly unlikely that reasonable persons will always arrive at the same conclusions.[30]

In advancing the idea or fact, as he calls it, of the burdens of judgement and of the persistence of disagreement, Rawls is making what seems to be a bold and innovatory claim. In reality, this is a restatement of a basic and still unresolved question. The problem is this: why is it that our attempts to reason with each other on moral and political topics more often than not produce disagreement rather than agreement? Rawls contrasts this situation with that of the natural sciences where the reverse is usually to be expected. In so doing, Rawls is inadvertently pointing in the direction of some daunting problems that seriously weaken his theory. The most obvious problem is that the burdens of judgement do not stop with substantive first-order disagreements. They also create the conditions for reasonable second-order disagreement about how to draw the line between simple and reasonable disagreement. It is not clear why science, on Rawls's account, is able to overcome the burdens of judgement. Is there an answer to this question that no reasonable citizen could reject? Furthermore, once the burdens of judgement are let out of the box, their effect is far-reaching. There is no clear argument why some reasonable citizens will not reject Rawls's understanding of the burdens of judgement. The answer is that Rawls, in effect, defines a reasonable citizen as a person who endorses the idea of the burdens of judgement for reasons that are themselves beyond the bounds of reasonable disagreement. There is a deeper problem here. Are we to expect that citizens will endorse Rawls's idea of reasonable pluralism for the same or similar reasons? If Rawls were to provide reasons that no reasonable citizen could reject as an explanation of reasonable pluralism, then it would also be possible to ask for further explanation of that, and so on indefinitely.[31]

Rawls, clearly influenced by Berlin and, probably to a lesser degree by Weber, refers to pluralism as a central problem for modern political theory. However, Rawls shifts the emphasis away from a concern with a defence of the idea of value pluralism as a philosophical theory of value and moves towards an engagement with what he takes to be the separate and distinct problem of endemic political and moral disagreement. He does so, he argues, because the theory of value pluralism is a controversial theory. If this is so, it can be argued that although Rawls does refer to Berlin, especially when agreeing with his view that there is an inevitably 'limited social space' so that 'any system of social institutions is limited in the range of values it can accommodate', this is the only real sense in which he and Berlin share an understanding of the problem of pluralism.[32] The controversial nature of any philosophical theory of value pluralism stands in the way of it receiving Rawls's endorsement. However, it is not at all clear that the idea of the burdens of judgement is any less controversial an idea or that it can be so easily detached from the theory of value pluralism. There is another fundamental difference here that separates Rawls from both Berlin and Weber in their views of the nature of pluralism. Rawls's central and explicit concern, unlike theirs, is to contain and control it. The obvious but rarely asked question is: why? What is so bad or unwelcome about pluralism and political disagreement? Clearly, a central part of any answer would be that Rawls's basic commitment is to the search for stability and reconciliation in modern pluralist societies.

The problem here is that Rawls does not provide either an argument or much general support for his reliance upon the concept of stability. Rawls does not use the idea of stability to refer to the structure of institutions. Instead, he uses it to describe the way in which citizens hold their moral principles. He offers no convincing evidence or argument that stability in his sense is the normal product of citizens acting on their moral principles when they believe that their political institutions are founded upon the those same principles. Nor does he offer convincing evidence that stability as he defines it, is necessary for the normal functioning of liberal states.[33]

Larmore has argued that there is a deep confusion in the debates about pluralism. In his view, the basic problem here is best described in terms of the challenge of reasonable disagreement rather than of pluralism. Although he does accept the truth of pluralism, he argues that the kind of political liberalism that he and Rawls want to endorse cannot be bound to such a controversial doctrine. As far as Larmore is concerned, it is a mistake to believe that liberalism must accept as part of its rationale the truth of pluralism. Clearly, political liberalism as defined by Rawls and Larmore cannot rest upon acceptance of the essentially controversial idea of pluralism because, if it does, then in itself it becomes a highly controversial doctrine. Unfortunately for the proponents of this theory, it has become increasingly difficult to hold on to this notion. Indeed, Larmore himself hints that he too fears this conclusion may be unavoidable, when he states that it is impossible to ignore the possibility that liberalism 'may necessarily be just one more partisan ideal'.[34]

However, pluralism understood as a theory about the nature of value has to be distinguished from the fact of endemic disagreement. The basic fact that has to be recognized here is that 'reasonable people tend naturally to disagree about the comprehensive nature of the good life'. There seems to be a contradiction between the idea of pluralism as understood by Rawls and as understood by Berlin, even though they are often thought of as being essentially the same doctrine. The essence of the idea that Rawls puts forward on this account and calls 'pluralism' is not a doctrine about the plurality of ultimate values, but is, in reality, a theory that attempts to cope with recognition of the inability of reasonable people to agree about the nature of the good.

The question is whether this distinction between pluralism as a doctrine and the reality of reasonable disagreement is persuasive. It is clear that Larmore's reasons for making this distinction rest, to a large degree, upon his attempt to justify a version of political liberalism. Larmore and Rawls both want to counter the threat of pluralism with political principles that 'to as great an extent as possible' reasonable people can accept, despite their commitments to a diversity of ideas of the good. Larmore concedes that although these principles of political liberalism might not be able to stand above every controversy, the idea of pluralism itself cannot be one of these principles because it is too controversial a philosophical theory. Political liberalism can, however, accept the idea of reasonable disagreement, including disagreement about the truth of pluralism. There is, however, an imbalance between Larmore's account of the distinctive features of pluralism and of reasonable disagreement. The essence of pluralism rests upon the idea that the moral claims and the forms of self-realization that we can respect are many. In Larmore's formulation, pluralism is a claim about the sources of value. The pluralist differs from the monist in holding that even if incommensurability does not necessarily imply incomparability, even resultant resolutions of value conflict can be the source of disagreement.

How is reasonable disagreement to be distinguished from pluralism? In Larmore's view, there is a close relationship between liberalism and the expectation of reasonable disagreement. Modern liberalism, it is argued, has arisen in part in response to the idea of the existence of a disenchanted world, but, in contrast to pluralism, it does not endorse this image of the world but recognizes that it is an idea over which there can be deep and reasonable disagreement. The deeply disturbing idea that does have a specifically modern character is the recognition there is no guarantee that reasonable persons will agree on controversial question of ultimate value. According to Larmore's account, there has been a move away from the expectation of reasonable disagreement over religious beliefs during the last 400 years. This has broadened into the view that this is a relevant truth for all our ideas that are concerned

with deep moral questions. Modern politics and, more generally, modern culture have become permeated with the idea, to
use Ranciere's term, of the rationality of disagreement.[35]
Larmore appeals to Rawls's formulation of the 'burdens of
reason' in order to explain the existence of reasonable disagreement. However, he does not feel that this is entirely credible
as these 'burdens' are themselves not peculiar to reasoning
about values. Larmore is not altogether persuasive in singling
out the variety of experiences available in the complex division
of labour in modern society as of particular relevance in making
sense of the supposed increase in the propensity to disagreement. After all, it is not at all clear what kind of evidence
could support such an intuitive claim. Furthermore, Larmore
resorts to a strong constructivist interpretation of the nature
of science in support of his account of the fact of disagreement.
In order to strengthen his case, Larmore turns the question
around so that we ought to be asking why there is agreement
rather than disagreement in human affairs. Looked at in this
light, it is the high degree of agreement since the sixteenth and
seventeenth centuries among natural scientists that requires
special explanation, rather than the earlier and, presumably
more natural, forms of disagreement about nature. Although
Larmore accepts that the high degree of agreement among
natural scientists cannot ignore the argument that this is
brought about because they are, in some sense, 'on the track
of truth', at the same time he wonders whether it might also
be true to say that scientific truth is 'not simply what a community of investigators will accept when they agree to subject
their observation of nature to forms of reasoning designed to
secure agreement'.[36] In other words, Larmore's default position
is the persistence of endemic disagreement. There seems to be
no convincing explanation for disagreement, but we can certainly recognize it when we see it. However, there is no doubt
that the main reason why Larmore wants to distinguish reasonable disagreement from pluralism is that the latter is too controversial an idea to be associated with his support for political
liberalism.

This attempt to separate pluralism from reasonable disagreement is not compelling. If we point to Rawls's 'burdens of
reason' argument in order to identify the sources of disagreement, then it would appear that this clean separation of the

two principles cannot be made as easily as he implies. At least three of the 'burdens of reason' overlap with some fundamental aspects of pluralism. The unsuccessful attempt to separate reasonable disagreement from the idea of pluralism is another example of the difficulty, if not impossibility, of the attempt typically made by political liberals to exclude controversial comprehensive doctrines from the public domain. Political liberals such as Rawls and Larmore accept as a fact the sheer impossibility of finding agreement between radically opposed comprehensive doctrines. Their response, generally, is to exclude considerations derived from such doctrines from the political domain.

How convincing is this distinction between pluralism and disagreement? The problem here is that the thesis of the burdens of reason cannot be clearly separated from the theory of value pluralism and, even if it could, it remains an idea that is no less controversial. Larmore's argument for the existence of a clear-cut distinction between value pluralism and reasonable disagreement does not succeed. At least three of the 'burdens of reason' that Rawls sees as responsible for the persistence of disagreement overlap with some of the central themes of Berlin's idea of value pluralism. For example, Galston mentions the difficulties of commensuration and comparison, different kinds of normative considerations involved in the consideration of a question, and the difficulty of setting priorities and weights between values. Galston is right to point out that the persistence of reasonable disagreement that Rawls and Larmore see as inevitable often presupposes, and cannot be neatly separated from, the existence of value pluralism. [37]

It is clear that Rawls's term 'the fact of reasonable pluralism' refers to more than a straightforward brute fact. This so-called 'fact' is bound up with a theory about the causes of disagreement between comprehensive doctrines. The proposition that disagreement is permanent and reasonable in a democratic and open society is controversial. If accepted as true, it does not in itself tell us how we ought to appreciate this fact. Indeed, it is reasonable to argue that the idea that disagreement is permanent and reasonable is the central claim in Rawls's theory.[38] On close inspection, there are two controversial epistemological ideas contained in the burdens of judgement idea. One is that there can be no long-run convergence of the basic and essential ideas of philosophical, moral and religious doctrines. This has obvious political implications. This non-convergence thesis is accompanied by the second thesis of equal reasonableness. This claims that there is a plurality of reasonable but incompatible comprehensive doctrines.

It might be helpful to think about the ideas of pluralism put forward by Berlin, Rawls and others as belonging to a family of theories. There are overlapping concerns between them, but there are also clear differences of purpose and meaning in the way in which they are discussed. Berlin's and Rawls's contrasting conceptions of pluralism indicate differences of aim and of theory. There are two other points to be made here. The first is that we ought not to assume that the idea of the 'burdens of reason' is itself uncontroversial and not open to fundamental disagreement. In order to understand what is at stake, some appreciation of the distinct nature of Rawls's theory of political liberalism is necessary. Here the difference of aim and purpose is clear. Berlin, Galston and Gray all see value pluralism in terms of a metaphysical thesis about the nature of value. This, in turn, must have serious implications for the way in which we think about the tasks of political theory. Political liberals such as Rawls and Larmore want to redirect our attention away from this idea and to think of pluralism more as an epistemic thesis about disagreement that does not rest upon controversial claims about the nature of value. At the same time, the intention is to construct a distinctly political theory that steers clear, as much as is possible, of controversial philosophical ideas. Whether this is possible or even desirable is an open question.

In brief, Rawls's answer to 'the fact of pluralism' comes in the form of an attempt to offer what he calls a 'freestanding' political conception that does not itself rely upon any 'comprehensive moral or political doctrine'. Appealing to his concepts of 'an overlapping consensus' and of 'public reason', he defends his version of a liberal constitutional order by defining a highly circumscribed 'domain of the political'. The fundamental postulate upon which Rawls's account rests is that in itself it is not and ought not to be thought of as just another controversial 'comprehensive doctrine'. Needless to say, Rawls's critics have not been convinced.[39] One of the controversial and puzzling aspects of Rawls's strategy that many of his critics have pointed to is that he bars himself from claiming truth for his own theory because that would be to make a controversial moral and epistemological claim.[40]

In his reformulation of his theory of justice, which he calls 'political liberalism', Rawls argues that its central problem can be expressed in terms of the question: 'How is it possible that there may exist over time a stable and just society of free and equal citizens profoundly divided by reasonable religious, philosophical, and moral doctrines?'[41] Modern liberalism is exceptional as a political theory for its recognition of the centrality of this problem. In this sense, perhaps, there is truth in the idea that liberalism is, more than any other doctrine, the political theory of modernity if we agree that it and value pluralism are inseparable. The basic problem is generated by the fact that there are 'two characteristically modern phenomena' that are central for liberal political theory: 'the pluralism of ideals of the good life and the existence of reasonable disagreement about which ideals are preferable'.[42]

Pluralism for Rawls is 'a fact about free institutions'. Throughout the history of liberalism, a central concern has been to set moral limits to the power of government. It is not surprising, therefore, that Rawls states that a second fact must be considered. This is 'that only the oppressive use of state power can maintain a continuing common affirmation of one comprehensive religious, philosophical, or moral doctrine'. Rawls refers to a similarity between his theory and the view which Judith Shklar called the 'liberalism of fear': liberalism founded upon a basic fear of oppressive state power that could license policies of cruelty towards its citizens.[43] The 'fact of oppression' would be a threat even in what Rawls considers to be a 'reasonable comprehensive philosophical and moral doctrine' such as utilitarianism or the liberalism of either Kant or Mill, were they to be the doctrines affirmed politically. A society that required the affirmation of an 'ethical liberalism' of, for example, a Kantian or Millian kind, would still require the oppressive use of state power in order to maintain itself while, presumably, political liberalism would not.[44]

Rawls relies, without offering any supporting evidence, upon the idea that the political culture of a 'reasonably stable democratic society' will contain 'certain fundamental intuitive ideas' which can provide the basis for a 'political conception of justice'.[45] If citizens are divided by reasonable religious and moral doctrines, how are they to coexist as free citizens in a just and stable society? This is an especially difficult question when the relevant doctrines are not liberal doctrines. Is it possible for such doctrines to accept and support a democratic and constitutional regime? It is not sufficient that they do so on the basis of a modus vivendi, but rather as part of what Rawls calls an 'overlapping consensus'. It is essential for Rawls's concept of political liberalism that citizens who hold to non-liberal comprehensive doctrines 'endorse an institutional structure satisfying a liberal political conception of justice with its own intrinsic political ideals and values, and when they are not simply going along with it' as a result of the balance of power within their society.[46]

The difficulty for Rawls's idea of political liberalism is that he does not want to replace the comprehensive views of reasonable pluralism or to provide them with a true foundation, but, instead, to construct a 'conception of political justice for a constitutional democratic regime that the plurality of reasonable doctrines . . . might endorse'.[47] This means that citizens in such a state must endorse both their own comprehensive doctrine and what he calls a political conception which would be available to all. The basic worry here is that political liberalism cannot itself avoid being another controversial comprehensive doctrine, 'another controversial and partisan vision of the good life'. If this is so, then political liberalism 'may necessarily be just one more partisan ideal' and 'unless the modern experience is to dissolve in the light of the one irresistible, all-encompassing Good, our political future will indeed be one "where ignorant armies clash by night"'.[48] Despite the appeal to this dramatic imagery, there is no good reason to accept this description of our fate even if political liberalism is in reality nothing other than another partisan ideal. Political liberalism is unable, in its own terms, to convince us, however sympathetic we might be to its aims, that in itself it can be anything other than a comprehensive and controversial doctrine. There seems to be an implicit acceptance of a version of value pluralism that is shaped by the nightmare of a world of plural and conflicting values in which the operation of reason is severely constrained.

2 Reconciliation through Public Reason

Rawls put forward 'three main ideas' whose function is to defend the central claims of political liberalism. These are: (1) the idea of an overlapping consensus; (2) the priority of right over ideas of the good; and (3) the idea of public reason. Of these, the explication of the idea of 'public reason' is a significant and central innovation in Rawls's later work. Nevertheless, it ought to be recognized that this does not mark as sharp a break in Rawls's political thought as is often claimed. For example, the idea of public reason is implicit in the role that the concept of 'publicity' plays in the contractarian argument of *A Theory of Justice*. This is made especially clear in the way in which the idea of public reason is incorporated into the later restatement of the theory of justice.[49]

If any concept plays a central role in Rawls's later development of the theory of 'political liberalism', it is 'public reason'. It is 'not one political value among others. It envelops all the different elements that make up the ideal of a constitutional democracy, for it governs "the political relation" in which we ought to stand to one another as citizens'.[50] Many, however, have seen this as a retrograde step.[51] In the eyes of some critics, Rawls's appeals to the authority of public reason often allow it to serve as a 'magical incantation' that advances partisan causes as if they flow naturally from impartial reason. The use of the concept of public reason, it is argued, gives a false appearance of standing above or apart from the clash of conflicting values, tragic choices and intractable problems that characterize the political world.[52] In the same vein, Sheldon Wolin, in his close reading of Rawls's texts, describes public reason as 'the general will in an age of academic liberalism'.[53] It has also been taken as an admission by Rawls that he had given up on the idea of a 'well ordered society' that he had advanced in his earlier work. Nevertheless, those more sympathetic to Rawls's later work have thought it important to clarify and defend the concept. It is clear that the appeal to a concept of public reason plays a central role in his response to the problem of pluralism. The appeal to public reason rests upon a stark dualism that provides the background worry throughout Rawls's work. Public reason is presented as the only reasonable and fair alternative to politics as a form of warfare. It is too easy to settle for the fact, according to Rawls, that:

> much political debate betrays the marks of warfare. It consists in rallying the troops and intimidating the other side, which must now increase its efforts or back down. In all this one may find the thought that to have character is to have firm convictions and be ready to proclaim them defiantly to others. To be is to confront.[54]

The idea of public reason is introduced by Rawls as the alternative to this stark view and, one might add, parody of 'realism'. Public reason, it is argued, puts into the foreground the 'great values' that a society can realize through the cooperative virtues of fairness and reasonableness. They are the 'political capital' that sustains the public life of a society where politics does not descend into the realist nightmare. There is a certain sleight of hand here. Why accept that the realist vision, as described by Rawls, and his version of public reason are the only two options? Surely, recognition of the unavoidable nature of conflict and disagreement does not rule out an appreciation of the causal role of moral beliefs and values in politics. Put forward as the antidote to the dangers of political conflict and disagreement, it is the weaknesses and uncertainty of Rawls's use of the concept of public reason that demonstrates, ultimately, the failure of his theory to offer a convincing and non-question-begging answer to the problem of pluralism.

Since the publication of his *A Theory of Justice*, Rawls's more explicit confrontation with the problem of pluralism led to some self-criticism. He argued that, among these failings, his earlier work had failed to distinguish clearly between the distinctive claims of moral and political philosophy. The later development of the theory is, therefore, termed 'political liberalism' in order to make it clear that it is concerned to emphasize the distinction between what he calls 'comprehensive moral and philosophical doctrines', on the one hand, and the specific demands of the 'domain of the political', on the other. Possibly in answer to those critics who had accused him of excessive moralism, Rawls argued that his version of 'political liberalism sets out to be an explicitly political theory rather than a moral theory which is applied to questions of politics'.

Specifically, Rawls argued that it is essential for his purposes to distinguish between a general moral and a strictly political theory of justice. Nevertheless, this has not protected him from the charge that it has not escaped from being a clear example of the 'political moralism' that pervades much of modern political theory. This is revealed, in particular, in the way in which he defines 'the domain of the political'.[55]

The idea of public reason is linked to the argument that there is 'a special domain of the political'. This domain is characterized in terms of two distinguishing features. The political domain is limited in its scope to relationships within what Rawls refers to as 'the basic structure' of society. 'Political society is closed: we come to be within it and we do not, and indeed cannot, enter or leave it voluntarily.' It also refers to those relations of 'coercive power backed by the government's use of sanctions, for government alone has the authority to use force in upholding its laws'.[56] In Rawlsian language, if we take the political to be a special domain, then a theory that formulates its basic values must be regarded as 'free-standing'.

According to Rawls, political values will have sufficient weight to override the values of other, possibly conflicting, domains, such as that of religion. It is an essential component of his argument that when conflict or disagreement occurs concerning what he refers to as 'constitutional essentials', then appeal ought to be made only to those political values. It is here, he argues, that 'agreement among citizens who affirm opposing comprehensive doctrines is most urgent'.[57]

This is a highly controversial and puzzling idea. How are political and non-political values related? In keeping with most forms of liberalism, it is clear that what worries political liberalism as formulated by Rawls is the danger of the power of the state being used to further the claims of one comprehensive doctrine at the expense of others. Under modern conditions of reasonable pluralism, such a doctrine is bound to be highly contestable and contested.

The distinction that political liberalism makes between the public domain and private morality is, in reality, difficult to maintain and is bound to be precarious and unstable. The idea that under democratic conditions political values ought to outweigh any conflicting non-political values is one that many find 'alarming'.[58] It is clear that this idea of Rawls is one that is itself an expression of a substantial moral viewpoint that puts the duties owed to basic institutions over all other commitments. If this is so, then political liberalism cannot avoid the charge that it is itself no more and no less than one more comprehensive doctrine. Furthermore, if this characterization of political liberalism is correct, then it is likely to find itself, at times, in conflict with the other competing comprehensive doctrines which are most likely to arise within democratic societies in which the effect of the 'burdens of reason' is most clearly in evidence.

Any attempt to draw a distinction between procedural and substantive values is bound to be controversial. However, Rawls's argument for political liberalism relies upon making this distinction. At the same time, political liberalism argues that the principles of justice, of equal basic liberties and the difference principle, cut across that distinction. Rawls argues that, in a modern democratic society, citizens 'realize that they cannot reach agreement or even approach mutual understanding on the basis of their irreconcilable comprehensive doctrines. In view of this, they need to consider what kinds of reasons they may reasonably give one another when fundamental political questions are at stake'.[59] Rawls's proposal is that, in the sphere of public reason, comprehensive doctrines that claim right or truth are replaced 'by an idea of the politically reasonable addressed to citizens as citizens'.[60] It is clear that in Rawls's theory a crucial move has been to balance 'the 'fact of pluralism' with a belief in the existence of a sufficiently rich common public culture. This common public culture consists of principles accepted by all as valid, as well as 'a public reason that can be appealed to as standards whose validity is, in spite of the fact of pluralism, beyond dispute'.[61]

For Rawls, the idea of public reason 'specifies at the deepest level the basic political values and specifies how the political relation is to be understood'. Rawls's thesis is a strong one. He states that:

> those who believe that fundamental political questions should be decided by what they regard as the best reasons according to their own idea of the whole truth – including their religious or secular comprehensive doctrine – and not by reasons that might be shared by all citizens as free and equal, will of course

reject the idea of public reason. Political liberalism views this insistence on the whole truth in politics as incompatible with democratic citizenship and the idea of legitimate law.[62]

It is now clear that the kind of well-ordered society that Rawls argued for in *A Theory of Justice* 'contradicts the fact of reasonable pluralism and hence Political Liberalism regards that society as impossible'.[63] Contrasting the earlier version offered in *A Theory of Justice* with that of *Political Liberalism*, Rawls argues that whereas he formerly saw public reason from the point of view of a comprehensive liberal doctrine he now sees it as 'a way of reasoning about political values shared by free and equal citizens'.[64]

The idea of public reason is the true context in which, as Rawls puts it, 'the political relation is to be understood'.[65] The critical nature of this concept is made evident when Rawls admits that those who are sceptical of or who reject the idea of constitutional democracy will reject the idea of public reason. Of course, it is at this point that we arrive at the limits of reasonable pluralism. If we, for example, see the realm of the political in terms of a relationship between 'friend and enemy', or in terms of an either/or membership in a particular religious or secular community, or as a 'relentless struggle to win the world for the whole truth', then there does not seem to be much that political liberalism can offer. This reference to those who see political life in terms of 'friend and enemy' relations, presumably a reference to Carl Schmitt and others with similar views, makes clear what for Rawls is at stake in this debate.

In his 1996 Introduction to the paperback edition of Political Liberalism, Rawls's underlying anxieties are made very clear. Here he argues that the:

> answer we give to the question of whether a just democratic society is possible and can be stable for the right reason affects our background thoughts and attitudes about the world as a whole. And it affects these thoughts and attitudes before we come to actual politics, and limits or inspires how we take part in it. Debates about the general philosophical questions cannot be the daily stuff of politics, but that does not make these questions without significance, since what we think their answers are will shape the underlying attitudes of the public

culture and the conduct of politics. If we take for granted as common knowledge that a just and well-ordered democratic society is impossible, then the quality and tone of those attitudes will reflect that knowledge. A cause of the fall of Weimar constitutional regime was that none of the traditional elites of Germany supported its constitution or were willing to cooperate to make it work.[66]

In Rawls's account, the idea of public reason 'belongs to a conception of a well-ordered society. The form and content of this reason – the way it is understood by citizens and how it interprets their political relationship – is part of the idea of democracy itself'.[67] The argument here seems to be this: modern constitutional democracy creates what Rawls calls 'the fact of reasonable pluralism'; this, in turn, requires that the values which underpin the relations between citizens and the state and between themselves are specified by an idea of public reason. Given the idea of reasonable pluralism, Rawls argues that citizens 'realise that they cannot reach agreement or even approach mutual understanding on the basis of their irreconcilable comprehensive doctrines'.[68] The point here is that Rawls's proposal is that, in approaching political questions, which are essentially questions of public interest, citizens appeal to a conception of the politically reasonable in place of their own comprehensive doctrines of 'truth or right'.

What does Rawls mean by 'public reason'? He states that:

> [a] political society, and indeed every reasonable and rational agent, whether it be an individual, or a family or an association, or even a confederation of political societies, has a way of formulating its plans, of putting its ends in an order of priority and of making its decisions accordingly. The way a political society does this is its reason; its ability to do these things is also its reason, though in a different sense: it is an intellectual and moral power, rooted in the capacity of its human members.[69]

What makes public reason public is that it is concerned with the public good and questions of 'fundamental justice' and that its content and conduct is public, that is, open to view.

The idea of public reason is clearly an ideal. It refers to 'how things might be, taking people as a just and well-ordered society would encourage them to be. It describes what is possible and can be, yet may never be, though no less fundamental for that'.[70] In using the concept of public reason, Rawls refers to Kant's idea of the public use of reason and the corresponding distinction between public and private reason. Rawls, however, is using this idea in a different way. In a democratic society, 'public reason is the reason of equal citizens who, as a collective body, exercise final political and coercive power over one another in enacting laws and in amending their constitution'.[71] One of the distinguishing features of this account of public reason is that its range of application is restricted to what Rawls calls 'constitutional essentials' and to questions of 'basic justice'. As examples of what this means in practice, Rawls mentions questions such as who has the right to vote, the limits of religious toleration, the range of equality of opportunity, and the right to hold property.

The argument is, that in order to cope with this reality and to maintain the stability of a well-ordered democratic society, it is necessary that citizens understand that when they face fundamental political questions they will only refer to a certain restricted range of reasons. The basic proposal that Rawls offers is that in the operation of public reason an idea of the 'politically reasonable' ought to replace all comprehensive doctrines that make claims to truth or rightness. Nevertheless, Rawls's idea of public reason must work with a distinction between reasonable and unreasonable comprehensive doctrines, as well as 'the fact of reasonable pluralism'. Reasonable doctrines are those that accept the idea of constitutional democracy governed by the rule of law. Those comprehensive doctrines that do not accept these political forms are deemed to be unreasonable and, therefore, open to criticism in a way in which reasonable doctrines are not.

Public reason is restricted in its operation to a particular arena that Rawls calls 'the public political forum'. This refers to the discourse and decisions of judges, the discourse of government officials and the discourse of candidates for public office. Rawls distinguishes between this idea of a public political forum and what he refers to as 'the background culture'. The idea of public reason does not apply to this 'background', by which Rawls means the 'the culture of civil society'. The background culture includes churches and institutions of learning. The non-public political culture, which includes the mass media, also serves to mediate between the public political culture and the background culture. In making this distinction, Rawls is attempting to forestall the criticism that the insistence upon public reason reduces and limits the scope of public debate. Nevertheless, this criticism that this idea of public reason does, in fact, constrict the scope of public debate does not disappear so easily. Rawls specifies an ideal of public reason. This is realized by government officials and candidates for public office when they act on, and give reasons for their actions on, basic political questions in terms of public reason. Citizens in general are to think of themselves as if they were legislators if they are to act in terms of the claims of public reason. This idea of citizens who ideally act on the basis of public reason and regard themselves from the standpoint of ideal legislators is an essential component of Rawls's concept of democracy. Citizens, he argues, 'fulfil their duty of civility and support the idea of public reason by doing what they can to hold government officials to it. This duty, like other political rights and duties, is an intrinsically moral duty.'[72]

What is the content of public reason? According to Rawls, a citizen 'engages in public reason . . . when he or she deliberates within a framework of what he or she sincerely regards as the most reasonable political conception of justice, a conception that expresses political values that others as free and equal citizens might also reasonably be expected reasonably to endorse'.[73] The 'fact of reasonable pluralism' introduces urgency into the question of how citizens are to come to an agreement over constitutional essentials and questions of justice when the differences of comprehensive doctrines may be irreconcilable. How are citizens 'who share equally in ultimate political power to exercise that power so that each can reasonably justify his or her political decisions to everyone?'[74] The answer that Rawls provides is framed in terms of the idea of reciprocity. Reasonable terms of cooperation are taken to mean that those who propose such terms do so on the understanding that it is reasonable for those to whom they are directed to freely accept them.

The importance of the idea of reciprocity in Rawls's theory is demonstrated in the way in which it is connected to the achievement of political legitimacy. The exercise of political power is legitimate when the reasons we give are those that we think other citizens might reasonably accept. This, for Rawls, specifies 'the nature of the political relationship in a constitutional democratic regime as one of civic friendship'.[75] Of course, as Rawls admits, it is open to us to maintain that when we are confronted by what he calls 'fundamental political questions' we are perfectly entitled to reject the idea of public reason. We then decide such questions in terms of our beliefs in 'the whole truth' as specified by our comprehensive doctrines. It is important to see here just how important the idea of public reason is for Rawls's attempt to deal with the problem of pluralism. Political liberalism must regard any insistence upon asserting 'the whole truth' in argument concerning political questions as being incompatible with democratic citizenship.

A central difficulty strikes at the roots of Rawls's theory. Political liberalism is probably unique as a political philosophy in claiming that its principles are not to be regarded as deriving from comprehensive moral, religious or philosophical doctrines. But political liberalism is, after all, as its name implies, a form of liberalism.[76] It is possible to envisage, Rawls argues, that under some conditions some non-liberal ideas can be integrated into its purely political conception of right and justice. The two curious examples that Rawls gives are those of the divine right of kings and dictatorship. This is, of course, highly implausible, but this example serves to make two points. First, that the political conception that Rawls favours is meant to be, in his terminology, 'freestanding'. If this is possible, then one could envisage a situation in which his political liberalism contained non-liberal conceptions. However, he suggests that such non-liberal doctrines could not be expected to survive within a politically liberal political domain. The second and highly controversial idea is: 'political liberalism moves within the category of the political and leaves philosophy as it is. It leaves untouched all kinds of doctrines – religious, metaphysical, and moral, – with their long traditions of development and interpretation.'[77]

The fundamental question that emerges here is that of specifying which reasons can be justifiably excluded from the domain of public reason. Rawls's concept of public reason is not concerned with the social domain. He claims this is an important point that is often misunderstood. It is not intended to restrict the range of open debate in the interests of political stability. Rawls argues that there is nothing in political liberalism to support that interpretation. But this is hard to accept. The idea of public reason as defined by Rawls is tied to a conception of constitutional democracy and citizenship. Here again the fact of reasonable pluralism makes this a difficult relationship. Citizens, according to the ideal of constitutional democracy, 'share equally in ultimate political power', but, given the fact of reasonable pluralism, differences between them 'arising from their comprehensive doctrines, religious and nonreligious, may be irreconcilable'. If so, then how are citizens to exercise their power 'so that each can reasonably justify his or her political decisions to everyone?'[78]

Although Rawls modified his initial view of public reason, the central idea remained intact. Citizens, under specified circumstances, are now allowed to argue on the basis of their comprehensive doctrines as long as this strengthens the ideal of public reason. He refers to this as the 'inclusive view'. In a well-ordered society citizens would, it is argued, have no real difficulty in maintaining the exclusivist view of public reason. However, in a 'non-ideal' society such as our own, which is not well-ordered or is, possibly, 'nearly well-ordered', a serious problem concerning the exclusion of ideas drawn from comprehensive doctrines can emerge. Rawls has given several examples. Suppose that there is serious dispute on religious grounds concerning equality of opportunity policy in education. Rawls's response to this possibility is to say that the leaders of the opposing groups demonstrate their commitment to 'fundamental political values' by showing in a public forum how their comprehensive doctrines support those values. This rests upon the presupposition that the common background culture supports a general recognition that comprehensive doctrines ought to be examined in this manner. Apart from the obvious circularity in this argument, it is far from convincing to say the least.

The case for Rawls's political liberalism is made more difficult by the challenge presented by the existence of a deep division over 'constitutional essentials' within a well-ordered society. An example that Rawls focuses upon is that of arguments for and against slavery in antebellum America. Here the abolitionists based their arguments upon religious grounds. Similarly, Rawls refers to the civil rights movement led by Martin Luther King. Rawls argues that in both cases the nonpublic reason of some Christian churches was in support of 'the clear conclusions of public reason'.[79] Martin Luther King was also able to and, in fact, did appeal to the values expressed in the Constitution 'correctly understood'.

It is often argued, too, that leadership in a democratic society must have something anti-democratic about it or that leadership is a necessary evil. In addition, ideas of leadership come into conflict with the idea that the liberal democratic state aims to replace the rule of men with the rule of law.[80] Perhaps the continuing existence of political leadership in modern democratic states and the high visibility of political leaders are some of those 'uncomfortable facts' that confront both political philosophers and political scientists. Nevertheless, it is worth noting that intimations of the significance of political leadership appear even in what would seem the most unlikely places. For instance, it is more than a little surprising to find that John Rawls's version of political liberalism contains an implicit recognition of the central role of political leaders at critical moments in political history. It is quite clear that Rawls, despite his central claim to steer by the star of public reason alone in order to avoid the charge that his own theory is itself no more than another 'comprehensive doctrine', has his own view of which particular leaders are his political heroes. Martin Luther King and Abraham Lincoln are two of the political heroes who clearly complement the contribution of his philosophical hero Kant in his own intellectual development.

What is it that Rawls finds admirable in Lincoln and King? One relevant fact is that they both stood up during periods of deep moral and political conflict for the values and ideals that Rawls himself believes are, or ought to be, the outcome of the free use of public reason. Lincoln's condemnation of slavery was, Rawls implies, an act of real political leadership in its refusal to accept the conventional 'communitarian' justification of that institution that was on offer at the time. Lincoln's achievement was, in Rawlsian terms, to set in motion a reconsideration of our considered convictions and principles on this controversial topic.

Similarly, Rawls takes his cue for the correct understanding of constitutional government from Lincoln. The significance of Abraham Lincoln among Rawls's political heroes is clear. One might almost say this is an example of uncritical hero worship.

Lincoln, it seems, can do no wrong. Even his Proclamation of a National Fast Day in 1861, Two Proclamations of Thanksgiving in 1863 and 1864, as well as the prophetic Second Inaugural interpretation of the civil war as a sign of divine retribution are, Rawls argues, not to be considered as violations of public reason 'correctly understood'. Martin Luther King appears in the text of Political Liberalism in a similar way, as a political leader whose civil rights campaigns Rawls enthusiastically endorses. However, in doing so, Rawls gets himself into a convoluted argument, the intention of which is to show that a controversial political leader such as King is acceptable because, after all things are considered, he did not really 'go against the ideal of public reason' that Rawls himself endorses.[81] Whatever the merits of Rawls's account of the role of public reason in political life, it is clear that the recognition of the significance of political leaders such as Lincoln and King, within a text which in other respects aims for a high level of philosophical abstraction, reveals something about the implicit intellectual and moral commitments that underpin his theory, as well as the convenient silences that persist within it.

According to Rawls's argument, public reason is to be understood in the context of the relevant historical and social conditions. This, of course, presupposes a political and historical judgement or interpretation of the relative significance of the many factors involved. In other words, the limits of public reason must be a matter of judgement. Rawls concludes that the abolitionists and the civil rights movement did not go against the ideal of public reason. He states that they did not 'provided they thought, or on reflection would have thought (as they certainly could have thought), that the comprehensive reasons they appealed to were required to give sufficient strength to the political conception to be subsequently realized'.[82] It is on this basis that Rawls accepts the value of an inclusive view of public reason.

The argument for the importance of public reason seems to rest on very weak grounds. It appeals to the more utopian rather than the realist element in Rawls's ideal. Rawls assumes that:

> the political conception of justice and the ideal of honoring [sic] public reason mutually support one another. A well-ordered

society publicly and effectively regulated by a recognized political conception fashions a climate within which its citizens acquire a sense of justice inclining them to meet their duty of civility and without generating strong interests to the contrary.[83]

Nevertheless, Rawls admits that his idea of a mutually supportive relationship between institutions, the sense of justice among citizens, and the ideal of public reason finds its support in assumptions about moral psychology that are far from being uncontroversial. Rawls himself points out that if these assumptions are mistaken, then there are serious problems with the theory. Nevertheless, the basic charge that Rawls is unable to rebut is that his idea of public reason and of the realistic utopia of political liberalism is, in reality, a highly partisan interpretation of American liberalism, presented as a universal, objective and moral necessity.[84]

Further evidence for the decomposition of the idea of public reason is provided not only by the modification of the original idea into the more 'inclusive' and 'wide' version, but also by the recognition that fundamental disagreements will continue. Although the vagueness of the proviso had worried some of Rawls's friendly critics, the recognition that disagreements can be expected to occur within public reason is even more unsettling. After all, in order to satisfy the requirements of reasonableness, Rawls had to admit that it would be unreasonable to deny there are other reasonable conceptions of justice. In fact, any conception that meets the criteria of reciprocity and recognizes the burdens of judgement can be considered to be a reasonable liberal doctrine. However, it follows that we have to recognize the existence of 'different and incompatible liberal political conceptions'.[85] It is a bit of an understatement to say that this feature of Rawls's theory has not been widely noted. It is also clear that Rawls did not dwell on the implications of this idea.[86] The basic worry is that the implication of Rawls's admission of disagreement into the public reason seems to undermine it. Therefore, it is not surprising that some political liberals have questioned this move as a move too far. If Rawls is as generous as he implies in the range of acceptable but incompatible liberal doctrines, then his own principles of justice are just one set among others. But the Rawlsian idea of public reason excludes any doctrine that does not accept his idea of fairness. For example, utilitarians and libertarians would find themselves outside the domain of public reason. It can be argued that this is not as damaging as it seems to be. However, this is not altogether convincing. For example, it is argued that utilitarians might be acceptable if they cling to an indirect form of their theory. But this is circular. It presupposes that they accept what they clearly do not in the Rawlsian theoretical apparatus that, in its attempts to preserve itself at all costs, borders on sophistry.

Discussions of the merits of Rawls's idea of public reason, while conscious of its many contradictions and shortcomings, often overlook just how controversial it is in political terms. Rawls, though aware of this fact, tends to downplay it. However, it is clear that when the political message is analysed, it can be nothing other than partisan and controversial. One central example is provided by the way in which the whole apparatus of public reason and related concepts is employed to argue for the superiority of one political regime.

A fundamental difficulty with political liberalism's reliance upon public reason as a response to reasonable pluralism is that it fails according to its own criteria of success. There is considerable scope for thinking that the use of public reason is just as likely to produce instability as it is to produce the stability that it aims for.

3 Kantian Republicanism and Political Liberalism: The Debate with Jürgen Habermas

The exchange of views between John Rawls and Jürgen Habermas is significant because it has disclosed some of the basic difficulties that contemporary political philosophy has encountered in its response to the problem of pluralism. Throughout the development of his work, Jürgen Habermas has been engaged in an attempt to provide a secure moral basis for a form of political theory that can support the central claims of western liberal and democratic thought and practice and, at the same time, to remain as far as possible consistent with the original spirit, if not the intentions of critical theory. Here one can often see a debate, both implicit and explicit, with the ghost of Max Weber, as well as with the whole German (and, more generally, European) tradition of anti-democratic and anti-liberal thought, which in this context is exemplified in the work of Carl Schmitt. The important question is whether, given his more recent attention to the problem of pluralism in modern societies, Habermas's idea of a discourse ethic that can provide such a foundation is not only plausible but desirable. In other words, has Habermas been able to exorcize the challenge of Weber's 'gods and demons'? There are considerable grounds for scepticism.[87]

Throughout the development of his political thought, Habermas has been preoccupied with a familiar set of questions and problems. This can easily be missed, however, because he has turned, with different emphases, to a vast range of diverse material and sources at different stages of this intellectual development. For example, in his earlier, and one might say more explicitly Marxian – or perhaps, more accurately, Hegelian – phase, Habermas directed his attention to the question of legitimation. In this instance the dialogue with Weber is at its most explicit. Habermas here, as well as in his later work, formulated a very strong claim. This is that 'the values and norms in accordance with which motives are formed have an immanent relation to truth [Wahrheitsbezug]'. Habermas continues by asserting that:

> [to] the highest stage of moral consciousness there corresponds a universal morality, which can be traced back to fundamental norms of rational speech. Vis-à-vis competing ethics, universal morality makes a claim not only to empirical superiority (based on the ontogenetically observable hierarchy of stages of consciousness), but to systematic superiority as well (with reference to the discursive redemption of its claim to validity).[88]

Put simply, Habermas's political theory rests upon what he calls an 'outrageously strong claim'. This is that 'there is a universal core of moral intuition in all times and in all societies'.[89]

This claim is made in stark opposition to Weber's thinking on the nature of legitimation and the theory of value that underpins it. From Habermas's point of view, the significance of Weber's account rests upon the fact that it forces us to consider the relationship between the justification of beliefs in the legitimacy of forms of rule (Herrschaft) and their possible 'factual validity'. Habermas does not dispute the usefulness of Weber's well-known ideal types. What he questions is 'the relation of legitimation to truth'.[90] This means, according to Habermas, that questions of the legitimation of political rule cannot be discussed adequately unless the truth claims made on behalf of such forms of rule are analysed and, if needs be, criticized. In setting out this problem, Habermas is directly countering what he takes to be the objectionable elements in Weber's idea of legitimation, which are, in his view, an inevitable consequence of his 'value-scepticism' and value pluralism.

Habermas is critical of Weber's account of this question, along with that of others, such as Niklas Luhmann and Carl Schmitt, for whom the practice of legitimation in the modern 'rational-legal' context is ultimately a question of the successful practical operation of a legal order. Furthermore, it has to be recognized there is an additional element here, which is especially important for Habermas. This is the question of 'decisionism', with its implied negative association with the 'radical conservatism' of the Weimar period. Although Habermas has occasionally modified this accusation when applied to Weber, the suspicion nevertheless remains that he holds him responsible to some degree for the development of this tendency which is in his eyes, ultimately, a form of irrationalism.

Similarly, Habermas has been critical of the understanding of the distinction between 'is' and 'ought', as 'critical rationalists' such as Karl Popper and Hans Albert have understood it. What Habermas finds worrying here is the way in which a deductive conception of practical reason has come to inform a non-cognitivist and decisionist stance. Although Habermas recognizes there is room in both Popper's and Weber's accounts for rational moral argument, they both are ultimately unable to escape from what he sees as an unsatisfactory 'decisionism' concerning questions of value. Habermas explains this in terms of the:

> narrow concept of rationality that permits only deductive arguments. Since a valid deductive argument can neither produce new information nor contribute anything to the truth-values of its components, moral argumentation is limited to two tasks:

analytically testing the consistency of the value premises (or the preference system taken as a basis); and empirically testing the realizability of goals selected from value perspectives. This kind of 'rational critique of values' in no way changes the irrationality of the choice of the preference system itself.[91]

For Habermas, the basic point here is that none of the prevailing accounts of the nature of moral value is acceptable from the standpoint of the kind of theory that he wants to advance. It is clear that the basic aim of Habermas's theory is to counter what he sees as the danger of a descent into irrationalism and decisionism by defending the idea that 'practical questions admit of truth'. If this is so, then Habermas argues that what he calls 'justifiable norms' express 'generalizable interests' and are based on a 'rational consensus'.[92]

In his later work, Jürgen Habermas has been involved in an exploration of a similar range of questions to those of Rawls. The problem of value pluralism has resurfaced in a more explicit way in his confrontation with Anglo-American political theory and, in particular, in his dialogue with John Rawls. In this later work, Habermas now seems to take seriously what he had previously, in his earlier writings, referred to, from a more Hegelian point of view, as 'the so-called pluralism of values'.[93] This is one good reason why the exchange of views between Rawls and Habermas is especially interesting and revealing of the underlying commitments and limitations in the work of both theorists.

Rawls and Habermas, although approaching the same set of problems from very different directions, do, in fact, share many ideas. The main difference, however – which Rawls argues distinguishes his position from that of Habermas – is that, in his view, his own position does not constitute a comprehensive doctrine; nor ought it to be thought of as being a part of a comprehensive doctrine. Rawls emphasizes that his theory sets strict limits upon itself. Rawls states this clearly: 'I think of political liberalism as a doctrine that falls under the category of the political. It works entirely within that domain and does not rely on anything outside it.'[94].

Habermas, despite his assertion of his essential agreement with the basic intention, project, and results of Rawls's work, argues that it goes wrong in several important ways. The original position, he argues, does not do the job that it was meant to do. Habermas does not dissent from the now common view that 'John Rawls's *A Theory of Justice* marks a pivotal turning point in the most recent history of practical philosophy, for he restored long suppressed moral questions to the status of serious objects of philosophical investigation'.[95] Furthermore, Habermas sees Rawls's work as directly renewing the Kantian tradition whose significance, for him, rests upon the idea that the fundamental questions of moral philosophy are capable of being posed in such a manner that they admit of rational resolution. If this is accepted, then the idea of a just society constructed on such a foundation is neither a mirage nor a utopia. One reason why Rawls's work is important for Habermas rests on his criticism of both utilitarianism and value scepticism. Habermas sees Rawls post-*A Theory of Justice* writings as expressions of an important rejection of the dangers of scepticism about the role of reason in moral and political life.

Habermas, however, does not accept that the idea of the original position is entirely successful in its task of clarifying a standpoint of impartial judgement. He argues that the attempt to gain a neutral standpoint takes place at the expense of its claim to validity. This is an important point for Habermas and for an understanding of the disagreement between him and Rawls. As a result, Habermas argues, Rawls's avowed aim of bringing 'the liberties of the ancients into harmony with the liberties of the moderns' fails. The important point here for Habermas is that the result of Rawls's argument is to give a primacy to the principle of rights over that of democracy.

A particularly controversial question in the debate between Habermas and Rawls turns on their respective concepts of 'the political'. For Habermas, as well as for many critics, Rawls's account, to a large extent, turns on his account of what he terms 'the domain of the political'. The whole point and possible success of his strategy of creating a 'freestanding' conception of 'justice as fairness' depends upon what is and what is not included in the political domain. For Habermas, the crucial question here is the nature of the contrast that Rawls makes between 'the political' and 'the metaphysical'. How is it possible to argue for the epistemic status of the freestanding view of political theory without stepping outside the narrowly defined 'domain of the political'? Habermas recognizes that, given the 'fact of pluralism', it is a legitimate task for a political theory to attempt to achieve a consensus across comprehensive doctrines. However, 'it does not follow that political theory can itself move entirely within the domain of the political and steer clear of stubborn philosophical controversies'.[96]

At the heart of Habermas's criticism of Rawls there is, despite the surface agreement, a sharp difference of strategy and outlook. The Rawlsian programme suffers from an unnecessary 'modesty', in Habermas's opinion. In Habermas's view, Rawls's commitment to the 'method of avoidance' has unfortunate consequences. Of these, the most doubtful is the idea of developing political philosophy as an autonomous discipline that avoids controversial philosophical questions. According to Habermas, this 'avoidance strategy can lead to an impressively self-contained theory', but 'even Rawls cannot develop his theory in as "freestanding" a fashion as he would like'.[97] Habermas draws our attention to what is, in fact, the quite remarkable nature of the claims Rawlsian political liberalism makes in its attempt to set itself apart from most other kinds of political philosophy, by avoiding arguments concerning questions of truth and rationality. Rawls has not shown that it is possible or desirable to avoid questions of truth and rationality.

Habermas and Rawls share a similar diagnosis of 'the modern condition'. Habermas recognizes and accepts that Rawls's political liberalism is an important response to the challenge posed by 'the fact of pluralism'. The problem is that, as Habermas points out, the requirement for political consensus on questions of justice cannot, under modern conditions, be based upon the existence of a society-wide established set of values. Despite this conjectured loss of social unity, Habermas argues that members of modern societies do continue to reason in terms of, and to appeal to, moral convictions that they assume ought to command general acceptance.

Habermas accepts an account of modernity that is similar to that of Rawls. Both accept a view that is influenced by the Weberian image of a disenchanted world. Reacting to this modern predicament, Habermas argues that 'moral philosophers and political theorists have felt that their task is to provide a convincing substitute for traditional justifications of norms and principles'. In traditional societies, moral norms and principles:

> were presented in the assertoric mode of statements expressing truth claims. However, with the public devaluation of religious or metaphysical explanations and with the rise of the epistemic authority of the empirical sciences, normative statements have become more sharply differentiated from descriptive state-ments, on the one hand, and from value-judgements and expressive utterances on the other . . . with the transition to modernity the 'objective' reason embodied in nature or sacred history was displaced by the 'subjective' reason of the human mind. With this there arose the question of whether normative statements retain any cognitive content and, if so, how can they be justified.[98]

Rawls and Habermas are alike in that both seek to steer a course that rejects both moral realism and value scepticism. Both accept and, in different ways, take their observation of a capacity for moral judgement and for reasonable moral argu-ment as a basic fact of social life that must be incorporated into the infrastructure of any political theory that fully appreciates the condition of modern pluralism.

The question that Habermas raises at this point is this: what is the correct conception of practical rationality that we can appeal to in order to explain and justify normative statements? In order to answer this question, Habermas presents us with a dichotomy. He argues that:

> we can either follow the path leading from Hobbes to Kant and develop a notion of practical reason that in some way preserves the cognitive content of moral statements, or we can fall back once again on the 'strong' traditions and 'comprehensive' doc-trines that ground the truth of the moral conceptions embed-ded in them. Whichever route we take we encounter obstacles. If we take the former, we have to distinguish practical reason clearly from theoretical reason, but in such a way that it does not completely lose its cognitive force; if we take the latter; we have to cope with the irreducible plurality of worldviews that are held to be true within each of the corresponding communi-ties of believers, although everyone knows that only one of them can be true.[99]

Habermas's strategy has been to construct an idea of practical deliberation that draws upon the Kantian idea of public reason. In short, Habermas does not see any real alternative to the form of Kantian theorizing that he advocates. As a consequence, it is not surprising that he is critical of what he sees as Rawls's turning away, in Political Liberalism, from his earlier 'Kantian constructivism'. Rawls, of course, had to do this or at least appear to do so, as Kantian theory, which is now categorized as a controversial comprehensive doctrine, cannot serve as a justification for political liberalism. For Habermas, the method of reflective equilibrium that Rawls introduced in his *A Theory of Justice* can be reinterpreted as a way out of the impasse, as he sees it, of the theory of political liberalism. This impasse or 'dead end', as Habermas calls it, emerges from the way in which the relationship between the political philosopher and the citizen is envisaged in political liberalism.

The tension which Habermas points to in Rawls's account is between 'the reasonableness of a political conception acceptable to all citizens with reasonable comprehensive doctrines and the truth that individuals ascribe to this conception from within their respective comprehensive views'.[100] This way of putting the problem highlights a range of basic questions which are raised in the elaboration of political liberalism, but which are never satisfactorily answered. The political conception of justice, which Rawls argues for, requires that it is endorsed from within the full range of reasonable comprehensive doctrines. Those comprehensive doctrines must themselves be consistent with the standards of practical reason. The question here is: what makes these doctrines reasonable? Habermas's suggestion is that the attempt to provide an answer lands Rawls in a dilemma. Either Rawls's recognition of the problem of pluralism which propels the argument of political liberalism means that he has to abandon the 'Kantian interpretation' which he had proposed in *A Theory of Justice*, or he has to abandon the distinction between the political and the metaphysical that he has made central to his theory.

Habermas's discussion of Rawls's political liberalism exposes the problems and tensions not only in Rawls's but in his own attempt to construct a political theory which is an appropriate response to what they both agree are the essential features of 'the modern condition'. The question to which Habermas directs our attention is, on the surface, a simple one. Who has the last word on the question of justification – the citizens or the philosopher? According to Habermas, the ultimate arbiters must be citizens. The framework for their judgements is bound to be the reasonable comprehensive doctrines that they hold. If they were not, then Rawls's theory would contradict its own liberalism because it would be prejudging the outcome of the deliberation of citizens. The danger that Habermas hints at is that Rawlsian political liberalism can easily become a form of paternalism. Rawls could, of course, reply that this is to misunderstand the idea of reflective equilibrium.

This tension in Rawls's political liberalism shows itself in the way in which an appeal is made to both the idea of an objective point of view and to the idea of a reflective equilibrium that draws upon the background political culture of the liberal democratic state. On the one hand, 'the philosopher observes standards of rationality that have a moral-practical content though they are independent of any comprehensive doctrine. Whether these standards at the same time impose limitations on the comprehensive doctrines of reasonable citizens depends on how one understands the philosopher's task.'[101] Is Rawls saying that the philosopher delivers an objective view to which citizens accommodate their comprehensive doctrines or, given the egalitarianism of the theory, is the philosopher just one citizen among others who must take his or her chances in open debate? On the other hand, the method of reflective equilibrium seems to imply that the task of the political philosopher is, ultimately, to make explicit the basic ideas and principles which are taken to be implicit within the public political culture. One difficult problem arises here when the public culture itself is 'divided at a very deep level' and would, at the least, imply considerable problems of interpretive disagreement.[102] Nevertheless, the basic idea is that an affinity is presupposed between the relevant political philosophical theory and the political culture. As far as Habermas is concerned, an additional critical component must be added. It is not sufficient to say that the task of political philosophy is to explicate the ideas and concepts that are embedded in the background public political culture. An acceptable political philosophy must be able to judge the claims made within a particular political culture. This implies the existence of standards for a rational conception of justice. The dilemma is that, under modern conditions of pluralism, a viable political philosophy must 'avoid equally the uncritical affirmation of the status quo and the assumption of a paternalistic role. It should neither simply accept established traditions nor construct a detailed design for a well-ordered society.'[103]

Habermas argues that his own appropriation of the idea of a reflective equilibrium offers an escape from this dilemma. The route which Habermas charts is one which leads towards the position that founds itself upon the assertion that an impartial practical reason can serve as such a standard and, even more controversially, that it finds itself to be reflected in the development of 'society itself'. In fact, as evidence, Habermas cites the way in which modern societies find themselves criticized from within by the moral standpoints expressed by various social movements. The Hegelian element in Habermas's own political thought reasserts itself and is in some tension with his Kantian conception of public reason.

In order to make sense of Habermas's argument, it is important to recognize that he is working with a distinction between what he refers to as the ethical and the moral. According to this distinction, the ethical refers to what Rawls calls comprehensive doctrines. These comprise visions of the good and 'form the core of an individual or collective self-understanding. On the other hand, ethical questions are questions of identity.'[104] Habermas argues that they ought to be judged in terms of the authenticity of the 'self-understandings' that they create. According to Habermas, such ethical understanding is always context-dependent. Furthermore, it is to be expected that ethical disputes will generally produce some form of reasonable disagreement.

The point of the distinction between the ethical and the moral that Habermas makes is to support the argument that, while reasonable disagreement might be true for ethical judgements, this is not necessarily true for moral and, by implication, political judgements. In fact, Habermas makes the remarkably strong claim that 'we expect that moral questions and questions of political justice admit in principle of universally valid answers'.[105] This highly controversial claim is that moral questions which include questions of justice do admit of justifiable answers because 'they are concerned with what, from an ideally expanded perspective, is in the equal interest of all'.[106] What Habermas calls 'ethical questions', on the other hand, are not amenable to the same kind of treatment. Comprehensive doctrines, in Rawls's sense, are concerned with ethical questions and, in Habermas's view, cannot be understood in terms of their truth or falsity in a straightforward manner. If this is correct, then in Habermas's view, it cannot be right to make the acceptability of the concept of justice as fairness contingent upon the 'reasonableness' or truth of a comprehensive doctrine in the way in which he argues that Rawls, in fact, does.

Habermas is convinced, in contrast with Rawls, that his attempt to transcend the problem of pluralism must lead in a republican direction. He initially sets out the contrast between Rawls's political liberalism and his own 'Kantian Republicanism' in terms of the set of intuitions that underline the two theories. He claims that the central intuition of political liberalism is to defend the individual and his or her way of life from interference by the power of the state. Individuals must be free to pursue their own conceptions of the good. The basic point of public life is that it functions to support and protect the autonomy of citizens.

The foundational intuition of Habermas's 'Kantian Republicanism' is that the public use of reason, institutionalized in the form of democratic deliberation, must be the central feature of any legitimate regime. Habermas's way of differentiating his position from that of Rawls's political liberalism and from other forms of liberalism is, by way of an appropriation of Kant's concept of 'the public use of reason', to argue for the primacy of democratic deliberation in the construction of any legitimate regime. The idea here is that 'all members must be able to understand themselves as joint authors of laws to which they feel themselves bound individually as addressees'.[107]

What exactly does Habermas propose as an alternative to Rawlsian political liberalism? And how does Rawls respond to these criticisms? Although Habermas has come to define his position, in contrast to Rawls's political liberalism, as a form of 'Kantian Republicanism', it is, in its essential aims, a clear continuation of the 'discourse theory' elaborated in his earlier work. However, as a theory with political implications, it now situates itself as an alternative to other current positions such as political liberalism, communitarianism and most other forms of republicanism.

Rawls's response is straightforward and amounts to the charge that Habermas's theory, whatever its merits, is itself a comprehensive doctrine and as such is unacceptable. Rawls argues that Habermas's theory:

> is comprehensive while mine is an account of the political and is limited to that. The first difference is the more fundamental as it sets the stage for and frames the second. This concerns the contrasts between our devices of representation, as I call them: his is the ideal discourse situation as part of his theory of communicative action, and mine is the original position.[108]

The reply to Habermas's criticisms allows Rawls to reiterate the essentials of his position. Political liberalism, it is stressed, is 'a doctrine that falls under the category of the political. It works entirely within that domain and does not rely on anything outside it.'[109] This, of course, is the innovation that Rawls proposed in order to escape from the problem of pluralism. It is an innovation in that Rawls is proposing to reverse the whole history of political philosophy, which has always worked with the belief that its 'concepts, principles and ideals' are the outcome of what he calls comprehensive doctrines, which might be religious, metaphysical or moral. Rawls is arguing for a conception of political philosophy, which is, in his terms, free-standing. Most people reflecting upon the history of political thought are bound to see this as a remarkable claim. After all, isn't this connection with comprehensive doctrines one of the features that is generally taken to inform and to make political philosophy possible in the first place?

This response allows Rawls to clarify his own theory and to show how it differs from Habermas's proposals. As has been noted earlier, the basic problem with Habermas's position, as Rawls sees it, is that it is an example of a comprehensive doctrine. As such, it extends far beyond the domain of the political defined in Rawlsian terms. Habermas's political theory is embedded within a highly complex and controversial theory of communicative action. This theory, as is to be expected, is itself highly controversial.

According to Rawls, Habermas's discourse theory is, contrary to its claims and intentions, undemocratic. According to
Habermas, Rawls means that, while his freestanding political
conception of justice makes substantive claims that are similar
to those of Habermas, it leaves it 'entirely open to citizens and
associations in civil society to formulate their own ways of
going beyond, or of going deeper, so as to make that political
conception congruent with their comprehensive doctrines'.[110]
As long as these doctrines are 'reasonable', as defined by political liberalism, then there is no need to criticize them.

Habermas has, in Rawls's view, constructed a form of
Hegelian theory. It conforms with a Hegelian sense of logic in
that it is an example of 'a philosophical analysis of the presuppositions of rational discourse (of theoretical and practical
reason) which includes within itself all the allegedly substantial
elements of religious and metaphysical doctrines'.[111]

In response, in his need to argue for neutrality between
competing comprehensive doctrines or conceptions, Habermas
points out that Rawls refers to the 'political' in two distinct
senses. One, which is fairly conventional, refers to the basic
institutional structure of a society. The other use of the term
is epistemic in that it refers to the status, which a conception
of justice ought to have, if it is to function as it ought within
a 'well-ordered society'.

Rawls's political liberalism aims to be a 'free-standing'
theory. Again, Habermas points to an ambiguity in Rawls's
notion of a 'free-standing' theory. This refers to a condition to
be met by all candidates for inclusion in the 'overlapping consensus' of a well-ordered society and it is also, at the same time,
a property of 'the very theory that explains it'.[112] In other
words, Habermas is making the important point that Rawls's
use of a key term such as 'free-standing' is essentially self-
referential. If this is so, then Rawls's claim for his theory of
political liberalism cannot itself escape from being political in
the sense of being reliant upon a contestable comprehensive
doctrine.

One difficulty that arises in Habermas's theory concerns the
distinction that he makes between values and norms. This is
open to strong criticism. Hilary Putnam, for example, has
questioned the way in which Habermas has built such a sharp
distinction between values and norms into his political and

moral theory.[113] Putnam's criticism is formulated within the context of an assault upon what he considers to be the mistaken orthodoxy of much contemporary philosophy concerning the question of value. Putnam argues that at the heart of many of the conceptual confusions that plague modern social science is the still popular idea that 'value judgements are subjective'. This generally and uncritically accepted idea is combined with the equally false belief that 'statements of fact' are capable of being 'objectively true'. In contrast, value judgements are held to be incapable of similar objective truth. In the extreme case, the proponents of a sharp distinction between statements of fact and statements of value argue that value judgements are immune in some ultimate sense to the operation of reason. In Putnam's account, this idea of the existence of a clear-cut and absolute dichotomy between facts and values has been dependent upon an equally misleading dichotomy. This mistake has its roots in the distinction put forward by Kant between analytic and synthetic statements. In Putnam's view, the pervasive influence of these dichotomies has 'corrupted our thinking about both ethical reasoning and description of the world'.[114] In pragmatist fashion, Putnam's rejection of these hard dichotomies rests upon a view that he has argued for at length. Hard distinctions such as these are to be rejected because they prevent us from seeing that the practices of description and evaluation are 'interwoven and interdependent'.

It ought to come as no surprise, therefore, to find that Putnam is highly critical of the way in which Habermas has resorted to the sharp distinction between the concepts of values and norms that is present in his work, and especially since the publication of the *Theory of Communicative Action*. This distinction plays an especially important role in the development of Habermas's political theory, as well as in his attempt to insulate his discourse ethics from the problem of value pluralism.

Putnam points out that the concept of a norm in Habermas's account denotes a universally valid statement of obligation. This characterization of norms is bound up with a:

Kantian interpretation of the essential power of reason and communication. However, values are dealt with in a very

different manner. In keeping with his 'postmetaphysical' natu-
ralism Habermas distinguishes values from norms in terms of
their contingent relationship with different 'life worlds'. Values
are viewed as contingent products of the social world. Habermas
requires that we defend our values in the practice of communication. Habermas's argument is that although the values
that are able to survive in 'communicative action' are those that
are deemed to be legitimate 'there cannot be better and worse
in any sense that transcends the "life world" of a particular
group'.[115]

Working from this account of the best way to think of the
problem of value, Putnam has put forward some particularly
damaging criticisms of Habermas's attempt to deal with the
question of value pluralism. The problem here, according to
Putnam, is that Habermas is still ultimately, despite everything, caught in the grip of a set of beliefs that seem to owe
their power to the lingering influence of positivism and its
separation of fact and value. The problem crystallizes in the
question of how values that fall outside the domain of discourse
ethics are to be treated. This is, in turn, bound up with
Habermas's acceptance of the image of the disenchanted and
'postmetaphysical' character of modernity.

It seems that, given this particular description of modernity,
Habermas must be reluctant to ascribe any kind of objectivity
to values. The charge of 'positivism' must sound strange, but
insofar as it simply points to a suspicion of metaphysics then it
does point towards a difficulty in Habermas's attempt to come
to terms with the problem of a pluralist modernity. 'For given
a pluralism of legitimate world views, conflicts of justice can
be resolved only if the disputing parties agree to create an
inclusive We-perspective by mutual perspective-taking.'[116]
Indeed, Habermas asks how 'we modern pluralists' can answer
the question of 'how normative relations and conflicts can be
settled among collectives with contradictory ideals, "ideals of
human flourishing", given the premise that any rational genealogy of values is bound to the We-perspective of a collaborative
community concerned with its own common good'.[117]

Faced with the problem of pluralism and disagreement,
there is nothing in Habermas's later work that gets us any
further towards a coherent and plausible answer. Despite all
the technical and, some would add, confusing elaboration of

the foundation of 'discourse ethics' in the idea of an 'ideal speech situation', there is one glaring gap in Habermas's theory. This is the surprising failure to take political disagreement as seriously as he ought to, given his intention to bring his theory to bear on the institutional reality of modern democratic societies and to repair the division between normative and 'objectivist' accounts that he sees as such a troubling feature of contemporary legal and political theory.[118] Perhaps this is an inevitable result of theorizing at this level of abstraction. Theories of this kind become either so abstract that they cannot deliver any moral principles or, if they do, the principles are those that were built into the theory in the first place.[119] Throughout all of the twists and turns in the elaboration of his theory, there remains one basic idea. This is the belief in the possibility of agreement on fundamental political and moral issues. One cannot help feeling that underneath all of this conceptual elaboration there lies an article of faith in the redemptive power of reason. As one commentator on Habermas was led to exclaim: 'we are surely entitled to something more rigorous from our social philosophers than a continuation of Protestantism by other means'.[120]

3 History and Theory

Although Rawls himself states that it is no more than a 'conjecture', it is clear that his idea of 'political liberalism' draws upon a controversial interpretation of history. This interpretation, in turn, supports a view of the specific character of the modern predicament. The introduction of a philosophical account of history or, perhaps, more accurately, a genealogy ought not to be dismissed as an afterthought.[121] It plays an important and central role in Rawls's explication of his political theory. The theory explicitly presupposes 'a historical story'.[122] The way in which Rawls appeals to an interpretation of the facts, as he sees them, of modern history is meant to supply strong support for his proposed solution for the problem of pluralism. The four central facts of reasonable pluralism, democratic unity in diversity, public reason and the liberal democratic peace are, according to Rawls, confirmed by our reflection on history and political experience. Rawls goes even further to assert that they 'were not discovered by social theory, nor should they be in dispute, as they are virtually truisms'.[123]

The centrality of this historical account suggests that the rigid distinction that is often made between a seemingly analytically rigorous theorist, such as Rawls, and the so-called 'gurus' of twentieth-century political thought, such as Hannah Arendt, Leo Strauss and Michael Oakeshott, is not as reliable as it is often claimed to be.[124] Furthermore, the presence of this historical interpretation gives us some further clues towards an understanding of the sources and deeper concerns of the theory. It is also worth bearing in mind that we ought not to be surprised by this development. It is a mark of modern political thought that since the French Revolution and the collapse of confidence in the idea of nature as a foundation all grand theories of this kind are tempted to develop a philosophy of history as a substitute and support.[125]

Rawls's historical account has an affinity with Weber's vision of a modern disenchanted and polytheistic world. For Rawls, pluralism or, strictly speaking, reasonable pluralism is understood either as a modern problem or as a more pervasive problem that has assumed a particularly modern character. Rawls is in agreement with such earlier liberal thinkers as Constant in making a contrast between the ancients and the moderns in terms of the fundamental problems that political theory faces. According to Rawls, the modern world has been decisively influenced by three developments. The Reformation, the development of the modern state and the growth of modern science have each had the effect of undermining a shared belief in the nature of the highest good. Rawls accepts the view that one of the historical origins of liberalism is to be found in the long controversies in the sixteenth and seventeenth centuries over religious toleration. Rawls, it has been pointed out, accepts Weber's idea that the Enlightenment has not given us the rule of reason but an era of, at the extreme, conflict, disagreement and decision between warring gods and demons.[126]

Rawls, in his historical interpretation, seeks to highlight the specific nature of the political predicament of the western liberal democratic state. He argues that, while the moral and political philosophy of the ancient Greeks sought, unaided by the authority of a religious text, to explore the question of the highest human good, the turning point in the political history of the west can be identified with three developments. The first was the Reformation of the sixteenth century. Its main consequence was the fragmentation of the religious unity of the medieval world. The second was the resulting religious pluralism that was the initiator of the pluralism of belief that has become a central feature of the western world since at least the eighteenth century. The third was the development, from the seventeenth century, of the modern state with its characteristics of a central administration, allied with the monopoly of the legitimate use of the means of violence. These developments coincided with the emergence of modern science.

The significance of this historical sketch lies in the importance that it gives to an idea of the specific and unique nature of the modern western predicament. What distinguishes the modern from the ancient and medieval worlds is the loss of a sense of certainty in questions concerning the nature of the highest good. Thus, for Rawls, one of the origins of modern liberalism is to be found in the Reformation. As a consequence, 'political liberalism assumes the fact of reasonable pluralism as a pluralism of comprehensive doctrines, including both religious and nonreligious doctrines'.[127] For Rawls, and modern liberal thought in general, we have to recognize and, indeed, welcome, the pluralism of comprehensive doctrines as a natural consequence of the exercise of human reason operating under conditions of political freedom. From this standpoint, the liberal constitutional state is an important human invention because it creates the possibility of a form of life that is both pluralist and harmonious. There is a strong suggestion that the emergence of pluralism is to be understood as not just a contingent historical development, but as a 'providential opportunity for the exercise of the highest moral powers'.[128]

The controversial nature of this historical account is often overlooked in the critical literature on Rawls. Contrasting it with alternative accounts shows just how controversial it is and what an important role it plays in Rawls's theory. Sheldon Wolin, for example, has contrasted Rawls's 'genealogy' with what he calls a Madisonian conception of politics. This contrast is intended to show the important difference between the latter's concern with the development of a constitutional system of countervailing powers and Rawls's concentration on the political consequences of beliefs. Rawls's genealogy reverses a

tradition of liberalism that focused upon a pluralism of conflicting interests rather than a pluralism of incommensurable
beliefs.[129] Furthermore, it is also revealing that Rawls's turning
points are all bound up with changes in belief rather than with
the revolutionary changes of 1688, 1776 and 1789.

Rawls seems to accept a dramatic interpretation of the post-
Enlightenment disenchanted world that owes much to Weber's
account. It has been suggested that there is an affinity between
Rawls's appreciation of the apocalyptic character of choice in
modernity and that of Carl Schmitt.[130] Indeed, Rawls, discussing the Reformation, asserts that what 'is new about this clash
is that it introduces into people's conceptions of their good a
transcendent element not admitting of compromise. This
element forces either mortal conflict moderated only by circumstance and exhaustion, or equal liberty of conscience
and freedom of thought. Except on the basis of these last,
firmly founded and publicly recognized, no reasonable political
conception of justice is possible. Political liberalism starts by
taking to heart the absolute depth of that irreconcilable latent
conflict.'[131]

It could be argued that these historical ideas are not important for an appreciation of Rawls's political philosophy. After
all, do not political philosophers, who generally are not profes-
sional historians, often make historical observations that are
meant to provide some illustrative support for their theories?
But it seems that Rawls's historical sketch does more than offer
some interesting and illustrative observations. On the contrary,
the historical interpretation plays an important role in Rawls's
attempt to convince us of the value of his 'realistic utopia'.
Indeed, one could go even further and see that as Rawls's work
has developed it is possible to discern the outline of a philosophy of history.[132] Of course, Rawls is not the first political
philosopher who has presented 'a narrative cast as an argument'.[133] Furthermore, it is clear that Rawls reveals the deeper
concerns, the 'unofficial or implicit theory', that informs the
'official theory', in his reflections on recent history. Rawls, in
fact, states his anxiety about the fragility of civil political life
in dramatic terms. It ought not to come as too much of a surprise that Rawls in his later work was not averse to discussing
the problem of evil and the worthiness of human beings to live
on the earth.[134] For example, reflecting upon the collapse of
Weimar Germany, he asserts that the:

wars of this century with their extreme violence and increasing destructiveness, culminating in the manic evil of the Holocaust, raise in an acute way the question whether political relations must be governed by power and coercion alone. If a reasonably just society that subordinates power to its aims is not possible and people are largely amoral, if not incurably cynical and self-centered, one might ask with Kant whether it is worthwhile for human beings to live on the earth?[135]

Remarks such as these, that occur more frequently in Rawls's later work, are clear indications of the fact that, contrary to all of his claims, it is hard to deny that the theory of political liberalism falls within the category of 'partially comprehensive doctrines'. Political liberalism is supposedly not formulated in terms of any comprehensive moral doctrine, but does draw on 'certain fundamental ideas viewed as latent in the public political culture of a democratic society'. If this is so, and the content of a political culture is not at all obvious, then it is hard to agree that political liberalism does not include 'conceptions of what is of value in human life'.[136] Despite the avowed attempt to do political philosophy without metaphysics, the theologically derived problems of evil and reconciliation are clearly at the centre of Rawls's political thought.[137] Rawls states that his theory is motivated by two ideas. The first is that:

> the great evils of human history – unjust war, oppression, religious persecution, slavery, and the rest – result from political injustice, with its cruelties and callousness. The second is that once political injustice has been eliminated by following just (or at least decent) social policies and establishing just (or at least decent) basic institutions, these great evils will eventually disappear.[138]

The world in which these evils have been eliminated is his 'realistic utopia'.

There are, however, limits to the achievement of this utopia. In effect, Rawls agrees with those critics who point to the circularity in his account of political liberalism. Quoting Hegel's saying that 'when we look at the world rationally, the world looks rationally back', Rawls admits that reconciliation with our political world is an option only for those who want to be reconciled. Many religious and secular 'fundamentalists' do not want reconciliation on these terms and cannot accept what for them are the false doctrines of reasonable pluralism, political liberalism, and the spiritual emptiness of a politically liberal society.[139] One might also add that there are many political thinkers who would be surprised to be informed that they ought to be concerned with the search for reconciliation. Rawls's modest idea of the role of political philosophy as a component of the 'background culture' is, according to some critics, like 'saying its goal is hanging wallpaper in Plato's cave'. Most of the significant political thinkers of the past were 'untimely' philosophers who saw their true vocation to be challenging rather than articulating the ideas and dogmas of their own time.[140] Nevertheless, the realistic utopia of full publicity shares at least one characteristic with Marx's vision of communism. It is a society without ideology understood as false consciousness. Citizens free from ideological constraints, illusions and delusions accept the principles of justice arrived at in the original position and applied to the basic structure.[141]

It is clear that the implicit philosophy of history that informs the theory of political liberalism includes an account of the history of political philosophy. This account, as with any interpretation in the history of ideas, cannot avoid controversy. Guided by his concern with the reasonable and the rational, there is an evident temptation for Rawls to read the history of political philosophy backwards in the light of his own commitments. There is nothing wrong in itself for a political philosopher to use the ideas of past thinkers in ways that he or she thinks fit. However, Rawls's account of some of the central figures from the canon is revealing and instructive. For instance, there is a strong sense that Rawls sees the history of political philosophy as a story of progressive development that culminates in his own theory. There is also more than a hint that the theory of political liberalism will 'fix, once and for all' the basic rights and liberties of a well-ordered society.[142] The controversial and unstable nature of the idea of a secular public reason that seeks to exclude controversial religious, theological or philosophical doctrines is illustrated in the way in which Rawls is unable to give due consideration to the fact that the struggle with such ideas was a principle concern of most of the contributors to the canon.[143] For example, Rawls's discussion of Hobbes, whom he sees as the author of 'the greatest single work of political thought in the English language', is remarkable in the way in which he chooses to ignore Hobbes's theological assumptions as well as his materialist metaphysics.[144] Although Rawls's lectures on the history of political philosophy are very clear and informative, they cannot avoid reflecting the controversial nature of the author's theory of political liberalism and the way in which it is bound up with an equally controversial metaphilosophical account of the nature and purpose of political philosophy.

The centrality of the problem of pluralism, recast in terms of the idea of the burdens of judgement, serves as the implicit background to Rawls's understanding of the nature of political philosophy. Rawls, as has been mentioned earlier, argues that we must not overlook the fact that political philosophy is always written with a particular audience in mind. He is concerned, initially, with his own case. Here, the citizens of a constitutional democracy form the audience. This is an important point that has important consequences. What is striking in Rawls's account of the nature of political philosophy in a democratic and pluralist society is his understanding of its limitations. This is in stark contrast with the self-understanding of most of the thinkers in the canon of political philosophy, certainly from Plato to Marx. Revising his own view as expressed in *A Theory of Justice*, Rawls, in his later work, argues that a liberal political philosophy such as his own ought not to be regarded as a theory. Political theorists are not experts on a special subject as are scientists. In Rawls's view, political philosophy 'has no special access to fundamental truths, or reasonable ideas, about justice and the common good, or to other basic notions'. The most that political philosophy can offer in a democratic society is that it can help us to clarify our basic political ideas and judgements. In so doing, can political philosophy claim any special authority? The question of the authority of political philosophy is directly connected to the way in which we think of its engagement with the world of democratic politics.

Rawls contrasts his own view of the nature of political philosophy with another view which he calls 'Platonic'. According to the Platonic view, the role of political philosophy is to find the truth about justice and the common good. Once this has been found, a political agent is enlisted to realize this truth. Rawls cites Plato's philosopher kings and Lenin's revolutionary vanguard as examples of the belief that possession of philosophical truth provides the authority to shape political outcomes. According to the alternative democratic view, political philosophers have the same authority as any other citizen. Whatever claim they can make must rest upon the authority of the powers of human reason that all normal adult citizens share. Whether or not an argument or idea put forward by a political philosopher is accepted is a matter of the response of citizens. Political philosophy in a democratic society is, in Rawls's terms, a part of the background culture. As such, it has a general educational role and it can inform constitutional debates.

Conceived as a part of the background culture, Rawls outlines four roles that political philosophy can perform. The underlying theme in this account is that there is such a thing as the background culture and the main purpose of political philosophy is to strengthen rather than challenge it. This is, of course, a highly controversial view with which very few, if any, of the political thinkers that Rawls discusses in his lectures on the history of political philosophy would agree. Neither, of course, would many of those important thinkers, such as Nietzsche, whom Rawls chooses not to discuss. Rather than 'swimming against the stream' as advocated by both Weber and Berlin, the fundamental aspect of the vocation of the political philosopher in Rawls's view is to seek reconciliation with our social world.

The first role that Rawls confers on political philosophy is that of confronting political conflict and division in order to 'settle the problem of order'.[145] The second role of political philosophy is to provide 'orientation'. Rawls takes this idea from Kant to mean that political philosophy can help us to think about how we see ourselves as belonging to a society with a particular history rather than simply as individuals or as members of associations and families. The last two functions are closely related. Rawls endorses Hegel's argument in the *Philosophy of Right* that political philosophy ought to aim for reconciliation. Political philosophy, Rawls argues, 'may try to calm our frustration and rage against our society and its history by showing us the way in which its institutions, when properly understood, from a philosophical point of view, are rational, and developed over time as they did to attain their present, rational form'.[146] Rawls is aware of but does not answer the charge that this can amount to being little more than an ideological construction in the Marxian sense of obscuring an exploitative and unjust society with which we ought not to seek reconciliation. However, reconciliation is bound up with the search for a realistic utopia. Political philosophy, on this account, explores the limits of practical political possibility.

A strong criticism of Rawlsian theory is that it is essentially parochial and has directed political philosophy in the wrong direction. One reason for this, it is argued, is its neglect of reflection upon history, social institutions and 'the real world of politics'.[147] In some ways this is a little unfair to Rawls. The problem is not so much an avoidance of history and political reality but the way in which it is understood. This takes us back to the fundamental idea of the realistically utopian response to pluralism. Turning the question round, we could argue that the theory is not sufficiently utopian. Just as his interpretation of the work of the thinkers in the political philosophical canon is constrained by his idea of the nature and limits of theory, his account of the prospects for public reason is also constrained by some basic but largely implicit sociological assumptions. As critics and sceptics have not been slow to point out, Rawls assumes that there is a solid core of established social scientific understanding about how societies 'really work' that all parties in an original position or operating within the bounds of public reason could not reasonably reject.[148] For example, it is clear that Rawls does not consider the possibility that citizens could hold a social or political theory that did not accept private property and the centrality of the market.

The political and, therefore, controversial nature of Rawls's answer to the problem of pluralism is evident in his discussion of the range and relative merits of plausible candidates for consideration for membership of the class of realistic utopias. Rawls's own preference is for a property-owning democracy. This is the political system that he considers as most likely to realize the two principles of justice that form the basis of his theory of justice. Property-owning democracy is contrasted with a capitalist welfare state, laissez-faire capitalism, state socialism and liberal democratic socialism. However, when property-owning democracy is compared with liberal socialism Rawls prefers to stay neutral. The term 'liberal socialism' seems to mean for Rawls something like the proposals put forward by John Stuart Mill. The basic point is that the principles of justice that Rawls has defended can be realized in both systems. As a consequence, 'justice as fairness does not decide between these regimes but tries to set out guidelines for how the decision can be reasonably approached'.[149]

It is clear that, for Rawls, it is of supreme importance that we recognize it is the possibility of a realistic utopia that has the power to reconcile us with our social world. At the root of a political theory that is supposedly free from metaphysics there is a deeply embedded hope that the possibility of a realistic utopia that comes to terms with the pluralism of conflicting doctrines is somehow connected to 'the deep tendencies and inclinations of the social world'. If we are able, for good reasons, to believe in the possibility of the realistic utopia, then it makes sense to work towards its construction. This is the central task that gives meaning to political philosophy in Rawls's view. It is not an exaggeration to see it as a 'liberal godless theodicy of reconciliation with our world'.[150] In effect, Rawls offers us a choice between two worlds: one where his version of political philosophy is practised and another in which it is rejected and, as a consequence, does not really deserve to exist.[151] Rawls's vision of liberal politics and its ability to cope with the problem of pluralism exhibits a strange mixture of optimism and pessimism. On the surface there is an optimistic hope that pluralism can be tamed through the use of public reason and the casting out of the unreasonable. But, at times, a deeper strain of pessimism shows itself in Rawls's despair that a peaceful resolution of enduring political problems will ever be possible. He accepts that in political philosophy there are no arguments that will always prove to be permanently convincing. The attainment of what in Rawls's eyes is the framework for peace, stability and reasonable politics will always be precarious.[152]

Rawls's respect for Kant is well known. He clearly understood himself to be working in the Kantian tradition. The fact that he, like many other modern liberal theorists, continues to do so is odd in some ways. Clearly, one consequence of the success of Rawls's *Theory of Justice* is a tendency to reread the history of political thought in the long shadow that it casts. Rawls and those who follow him ignore the fact that Kant's contemporaries did not consider him to be a liberal at all. The idea of subordinating politics to a categorical ethical doctrine was considered to be a dangerous move and a potential threat to liberty.[153] Nevertheless, it is to Kant that Rawls turns, and what is often overlooked is just how deep that debt is. Rawls states quite straightforwardly that the 'central motivation' of his work is concern with one problem: 'the survival, historically, of constitutional democracy'.[154] Constitutional democracy requires a moral foundation that will serve as a defence against the destabilizing threat of pluralism. That foundation is supplied by a reworking of Kantian theory. However, Rawls also revealed that his understanding of Kant's moral and political philosophy includes an appreciation of its religious and metaphysical aspects. According to Rawls, these 'aspects of Kant's moral philosophy seem obvious; any account of it that overlooks them misses much that is essential to it'. If this is true for Kant, then the same interpretation can be applied to Rawls.[155] It seems that, after all, Rawls's political liberalism, while consistent with many comprehensive doctrines, is not as 'free-standing' as he wants us to believe. It finds its own foundation in a doctrine that has clear religious and moral presuppositions. This is a liberalism of hope as much as it is a liberalism of fear.[156]

4

Pluralism: Reconciliation and Disagreement

The precise meaning and significance of the idea of value pluralism will probably continue to be the subject of deep philosophical disagreement. Nevertheless, it seems reasonable to say that most of the more dramatic and extreme claims that have been put forward are far from being persuasive. For example, the theory of the existence of plural values, even if true, does not necessarily have the destructive implications for the operation of reason and rationality that are often claimed.[1] The fact of value pluralism does not in itself undermine the operation of practical reason. However, even if we remain neutral about the metaphysical arguments for the existence of plural values, it is clear that the way in which we think about the status of values and the relations between them does have important implications for political theory. This is not to overlook the fact that there can be disagreement about what the relevant values are and how they can be distinguished from each other.

A difficulty arises from the way in which political philosophers often run together at least three distinct themes under the general heading of pluralism. First, there is the thesis that values are themselves plural and, even if comparable in some sense, are incommensurable. Second, there is the problem of endemic disagreement. Third, there is a more general thesis about the context in which modern politics operates that can be captured by such terms as 'disenchantment of the world' or 'the disappearance of the markers of certainty'. A general and striking point about much contemporary theory is the way in which it seems to accept the general contours of Weber's vision of our fate as living with a pluralism of values in a disenchanted world, while, at the same time, trying very hard to avoid the pessimism and despair which he took to be its inevitable outcome. Much of modern political theory is, to a large degree, stuck in this dense conceptual net.

Investigation of the way in which modern political thinkers have responded to the idea of value pluralism has revealed a deep, if implicit, division. There is a currently dominant strand of political philosophy that favours the search for stability, agreement and reconciliation. Critics of that view do not accept that this is a plausible and respectable aim for political philosophy. Political theorists in the latter category accept the existence of pluralism and endemic disagreement, but they believe that it is neither possible nor desirable to construct a theory that aims to resolve the problem of plural and conflicting values. These contrasting attitudes can be reflected in a disagreement about philosophical method. On one side there is a predisposition to see philosophy as a problem-solving enterprise, modelled to a large degree on a particular understanding of the nature of scientific inquiry. The other side sees its true task as the asking of questions rather than as the supplying of answers.[2] In addition, there is a strong affinity between pluralists and those who favour what they regard as a more 'realistic' approach to political theory. This, in effect, equates with the distinction between optimists and pessimists in their attitude to the fact of pluralism.

The existence of plural and conflicting values and of disagreement is, of course, one of the reasons for the existence of politics in the first place. Concern with either the search for agreement or with the persistence of disagreement is understandable. However, either of these concerns can be developed in an extreme or utopian direction. A basic and unresolved question is whether it is possible to combine these two interests in one theoretical account without producing what would be in danger of turning out to be a facile synthesis, or whether we just have to accept the fact of the existence of a perpetual and irresolvable tension between these two accounts. On balance, it seems that the latter is the more plausible, even if unwelcome, option.

As politics does not constitute a natural kind and the 'conceptual framework of politics' is a 'highly complex abstract object', we ought not to be too surprised to find that the concepts of politics and the political have been used with different meanings and in a wide variety of contrasting contexts.[3] Nevertheless, although a search for the timeless 'essence' of politics is a pointless activity, we ought not to let this prevent us from trying to make sense of those practices and institutions that we conventionally think of as being political. Abstract generalizations about politics or any other domain of human activity, for that matter, might be attainable but they will be far from informative. They will not tell us what we really want to know. Political theory is best thought of as a set of possible answers to the questions that we find interesting and important in a particular time and place.[4]

Although the questions raised in the debates about pluralism do not necessarily apply to every aspect of the political domain, they do, nevertheless, go to the heart of some of our more fundamental preoccupations. In particular, one of the merits of taking value pluralism seriously, even if it turns out to be a false doctrine, is that it unavoidably leads to a consideration of the difficult question of the problem of persistent political disagreement. In particular, reflection on pluralism has contributed to the sense of unease felt by many with regard to the general direction that some strands of modern political theory have taken. This is especially true with regard to what is argued to be the apparent unreality or utopianism of much so-called 'ideal theory'. Theories of this kind have frequently been accused of the crime of 'moralism'.[5] This ought not to be too surprising. Thinking about pluralism is bound, sooner or later, to connect with what is probably the most basic political question: how are we to live together in the face of persistent political disagreement?[6]

It is sometimes argued that one of the main failings in debates about pluralism and disagreement, especially those that have taken place within a broadly liberal framework, is that they have had the unfortunate propensity to narrow our understanding of the scope and nature of politics. In addition, the modern concern with pluralism is connected to the sense that we live in a world where not only is there a marked plurality of values, but, also, a marked pluralism in the way in which we hold those values. This is sometimes referred to as 'disenchantment', but whatever name we give it there is a deep sense that pluralism under modern conditions has produced something new in our experience. After all, talking about it in such a self-conscious manner is itself a feature of this novelty.

This tension between the search for agreement and reconciliation and the recognition of the persistence of disagreement can be described in various ways. Reflection upon value pluralism has certainly contributed to a feeling of dissatisfaction with what is frequently taken to be the excessive moralism of much contemporary political philosophy. The injection of a strong dose of realism into our political thinking is taken to be the antidote to the perceived utopian character of much modern Anglo-American political philosophy.[7] This moralistic and unrealistic character of political theory has also assumed a peculiarly modern form, it can be argued, as a consequence of the academic professionalization of political philosophy. In turn, we can ask whether making value pluralism a central problem has also, too often, had the effect of reinforcing a one-sided image of politics. Is there a danger of politics being too strongly identified with the conflict of values at the expense of other significant factors?

The moralist view, especially in its dominant liberal form, is, according to its critics, guilty of at least three basic errors of understanding. First, there is a belief that all societies possess, at some level, a basic consensus. This is connected to a belief that a peaceful practical elaboration of that basic consensus is possible. This, in turn, is joined to the idea that we are obliged to reach such a consensus and that it is rational to do so, or, at the least, it would be good idea to do so.[8] A contrasting vision of politics and society has been amusingly expressed by Raymond Geuss. His idea of three men and a plank has been put forward, presumably, as an alternative to such constructions as Rawls's 'Original Position' or Habermas's 'Idea Speech Situation'. Geuss suggests that a more useful and realistic image might be that of three people struggling to stay afloat on a plank that will bear the weight of only one of them. In this situation, he argues, it does not make sense to talk about a common good. Looked at from this standpoint, much moralistic theory has the character of sheer fantasy about situations in which all three persons are happily rescued by a lifeboat.

Much moralistic and, in this case, much liberal theory is equivalent to saying that these three persons have a flotation vest and 'if each was a fish, they could all swim happily away'. The problem with all such thought experiments, it is argued, is that they are carried out without any useful reference to actual political circumstances. Furthermore, unlike both Rawls and Habermas, with their faith in the existence of the underpinning certainties of social scientific knowledge that informs the understanding of the participants in their hypothetical 'modes of presentation', this account makes it clear that, for those with a more sceptical outlook, if there is one thing these sciences have taught us, it is that there is very little, if anything, produced by them that they can legitimately claim as genuine and ideologically uncontroversial scientific knowledge. The political and social world 'is a large, unsurveyable, and extremely unwieldy object that seems sometimes to be hopelessly inert and at others surprisingly mercurial'.[9] This version of realism owes as much to Nietzsche as it does to Hobbes.

One response to this predicament is to attempt to construct a utopian solution in both theory and practice. It has been a constant theme among the more 'pessimistic pluralists' that the search for such utopias is a dangerous illusion.[10] However, it would also be a mistake to argue that utopianism is a problem for moralism alone. Both realist and moralist responses to pluralism have their utopian tendencies, in the sense of each implying in their own way the implausible or unattainable nature of an ideal state of affairs.

Realism is not immune from taking an extreme or utopian form. One example is provided by those stark versions of realism that see it as a form of Machtpolitik. Here, politics is regarded as being not much more than a sheer struggle for power within and between states. This, however, is not the stance of the modern realists in political philosophy. The modern realist response to moralism does not deny the power of ideas, values and ethical commitments in politics. After all, if the political world is constituted, to a large degree, by disagreement, conflict and the struggle for power, we can ask why we should bother with normative or moral questions at all. One answer, given by realists, is to point to the role that normative ideas do in fact play in the political world. In short, clarification of our normative opinions or commitments is essential and unavoidable, insofar as our task is to identify and clarify human possibilities in such a hostile environment.[11] It does not imply, therefore, that realism, in the sense given to it by Williams and others, means that we cannot ask moral questions. It is, rather, that moralistic political theory asks the wrong kind of questions.[12] Furthermore, it is clear that there is a strong normative stance underlying the views of most realists insofar as they, usually even if implicitly, put a high value on the practice of politics either for its own sake or as a means towards some end. For example, one such end is the development of the moral character of citizens and politicians that is often taken to be one of the effects of active participation in political life. The self-evident moral passion of many advocates of realism in political theory has even suggested an analogy with the fervour of religious sectarianism.[13] Similarly, it is not true to say that the moralists in political philosophy are unaware of the objections of realists. This is certainly not the case with John Rawls, whose whole rationale for engaging in political theory in the first place was his deep reaction to the horrors of the political history of the twentieth century. The problem is that the price moralists in political theory pay, it is argued, in their response to those objections is an avoidance of the conflictual reality of politics.[14]

If it is agreed that political disagreement is a permanent and defining feature of political life, then reflection on value pluralism, while not taken as the only cause of disagreement, will certainly contribute to the understanding of our political condition. A basic and continuing worry is that political disagreements might be resistant to the operation of reason. This is an anxiety that has permeated much of the political thought of the twentieth century. For example, Max Weber and many of the political thinkers of the Weimar Republic demonstrate what can easily ensue from the dangerous thought that only some form of decisionism offers the most plausible escape from this predicament. In that particular context, the popularity of the idea of living in 'a time of decision' deepened the feeling of crisis that seemed to naturally complement existence in a world of plural values. Furthermore, recognition that the normal operation of reason is more likely to divide than to unite us on important political matters must have a profound effect on political thinking.[15] While Carl Schmitt's stark opposition between friend and enemy can be a useful and even a necessary corrective for much of the narrowness and complacency that seems to be an occupational disease in some academic political philosophy, it is not necessary to follow him into what is, ultimately, a philosophical and political dead end. Nevertheless, it cannot be denied that his work has been seized upon to fill what many critics of liberalism consider to be an intellectual vacuum. The ideas of such critics are often suggestive and challenging, but, too often, they lack clarity and tend to dissolve into rhetorical formulae. Nevertheless, this can be regarded as supporting evidence for the centrality of the problems posed by pluralism. In particular, the charge that is often made by pluralists, and not by pluralists alone, that much modern political theory is guilty of avoiding those realities that are expressed in 'platitudes about politics' ought not to be ignored.[16] It is the central point of Schmitt's work, on the basis of his support for the Nazi regime, although it was not entirely original in this regard, that a fundamental and unavoidable quality of political affairs is the persistence of difference, disagreement and opposition. The problems raised by the recognition of value pluralism add another complex dimension to this set of problems.

It can be argued that it is an understandable temptation for political theorists whose job it is to think about political ideas and principles to exaggerate and pay more attention to conflicts of ideals and values, while paying less attention to the existence of what many would claim is the more fundamental and basic fact of the persistence of conflicts of interest. Nevertheless, it is a commonplace of social science (or, at least, it ought to be) that interests cannot be identified apart from the ideas that define them. Raz has argued that, just as it is a mistake to disregard conflicts of interest, it is also a mistake to think that disagreements about principles are necessarily at the root of the most intractable and seemingly insoluble conflicts.[17] It is important too, as Raz has also pointed out, that the tendency to overemphasize the importance of disagreements over principles may well be a part of a 'growing faith in some academic circles in the power of theory to provide answers to questions' and also part of a 'moralizing phase' that western states are experiencing. There is a double-edged danger here: that of either downplaying or exaggerating the significance of plural and conflicting values. Raz, for example, argues there is a discernible tendency to exaggerate the significance of disagreements about principles. It is also true that it is often in the nature of political disputes for participants to appeal to and amplify whatever principles are available that seem to lend support for their cause. Nevertheless, even if disagreement over values or principles is not the whole of political disagreement, it certainly is a central and unavoidable component.

Much of the discussion of the nature and place of pluralism and disagreement in politics has suffered from a tendency to either blur or ignore the distinction between moral and political conflict. For instance, many of the philosophical and conceptually sophisticated discussions of the pluralism and incommensurability of values refer, only in an indirect way, to specifically political questions.[18] Without attempting the unnecessary task of looking for some final definition of 'the political', it is important to stress that despite all appearances to the contrary 'political philosophy is not simply applied moral philosophy, which in our culture it is often taken to be'.[19] Furthermore, it ought not to be forgotten that the idea of applied moral philosophy is itself a controversial idea.[20]

Arguing that political pluralism does not necessarily imply moral pluralism is not to deny the close relationship between moral and political questions. The point is not to assume that political questions can or need be described automatically only or primarily in moral terms. It is important to insist that 'the domain of political positions is controversial in a primordial sense in which the domain of moral demands and appraisals is not'.[21] The existence of division, conflict and compromise is inseparable from the practice of politics.

One of the central and implicit assumptions in much modern political thought is that the idea of the possibility of providing a rational foundation for politics must presuppose some degree of agreement over 'ultimate values'. The next step is to argue that in the absence of such agreement the idea of a rational basis for politics must be either abandoned or drastically limited. Even if we accept that these are legitimate concerns, and even if we accept the diagnosis of the disenchantment of the world that seems to underpin so much of modern political thought, it does not follow that there is no place for the operation of reason in the theory and practice of politics. Nor does

it follow that value pluralism necessarily makes reasoned decision and agreement impossible. Nevertheless, given the persistence of such 'platitudes of politics' as recognition of the
oppositional nature of political disagreement, we cannot avoid
recognition of the fact that the political domain possesses significant distinguishing features. It is not necessary to fall into
the trap of over-dramatizing the tragic qualities of 'the political' in order to have a healthy respect for those stubborn political realities that many political and moral theorists often seem
happy to ignore.[22] Nor is it necessary to fall into the alternative
trap of expecting the operation of pure and unaided reason to
be able to tell us what to do and how to think politically.

The responses to pluralism illustrate the persistence of a
deeper dualism in our political thinking. This can be expressed
in the distinction that is often made between 'politics' and 'the
political'. Although there is no single agreed way to make this
distinction, it does point to a fundamental dichotomy in political thought. In particular, consideration of the problem of
pluralism is often connected to strong criticism of the perceived shortcomings of much, especially liberal, theory, on the
grounds that it has trivialized or diminished our understanding
of politics. The most important version of this rests on the
charge that, to refer back to Rawls's terminology, political
theory is too often more utopian than realistic. The claim is
that much of modern political and, in particular, liberal theory
has been guilty of avoiding rather than elucidating the nature
of politics in its confrontation with pluralism.

The concept of politics can be understood in many ways. We
can contrast an idea of politics in terms of a concern with the
construction of a constitution in the broad sense, as the construction of a regime or polis, which seeks and guarantees the
achievement of the common good. Clearly, it is possible to see
a tradition of political thinking from Plato to Rawls that can
be understood in these terms. On the other hand, there is a
style or tradition of political thinking that sees politics in terms
of the operation of power, the persistence of conflict and the
clash of ideologies. Political thinkers such as Machiavelli, Marx
and Weber would fit into this description. However, this observation needs some qualification. Many of the most important
political thinkers are not oblivious to the existence of both
aspects of politics. Such thinkers are interesting precisely

because they either seek to find a balance or despair of finding one between these two contrasting images of politics. Plato and Aristotle, the founders of the western political tradition, clearly illustrate this point. For example, there is clear evidence for this tension between two views of politics and of the corresponding relationship between philosophy and politics in Aristotle's *Politics*. There is a 'good' and a 'bad' origin for politics. In Book I of the *Politics*, Aristotle discusses the political nature of man and the unity of the polis in terms of its *telos*. However, in the later sections of the *Politics*, starting from Book IV, Aristotle outlines a more 'realistic' image of the polis in terms of the endless struggle between rich and poor.[23] Again, although this distinction is valid, it ought not to be made too rigid. After all, Aristotle makes a point of arguing, in his account of the 'good' origin of politics, that the gift of speech ensures that political men are unlike other animals in their ability to argue. Agreement in a shared language makes political disagreement possible.

Another way of picturing this contrast in our conception of politics is to look to the distinction that developed in early modern Europe between the 'art of the state' (statecraft) and 'politics'. The idea of statecraft is founded on the idea that the task of the statesman is to construct and preserve a just city. The other image, of politics, is that of the centrality of the practice of reason of state.[24] This is a dichotomy that is well represented in the work of Machiavelli. Thus, Maurizio Viroli argues that 'current languages of politics leave out important dimensions of actual and possible political action. They do not help us to understand political life, nor do they permit us to prefigure possible political practices worth committing ourselves to.'[25] He distinguishes between a 'realist' and a 'civil' or 'critical' version of political theory. Theories of the first type are concerned primarily with the description of 'actual political practices'. Theories of the second type are more concerned with what a 'true or just politics should be'. According to Viroli, the view of politics as statecraft, as essentially concerned with the struggle for power within and between states, has become the dominant view. In addition, there is a distinction here between an idea of the theorist as a civil philosopher whose task is to advise on the best way to create and preserve justice in his or her city, and that of the theorist as a person whose less popular role is to remind us that politics is also about conflict and the struggle for power. In order to preserve our city, we might have to act unjustly or to preserve injustices. According to the implicit theory underlying these two views, the first assumes that despite the manifest plurality of values it is still possible to appeal to a latent and more coherent and harmonious political tradition. In contrast, the opposing view does not accept this understanding of the nature of the political tradition. This difference between what we can call the realistic and the moralistic visions of politics can be drawn in contrasting ways. However, the basic point is that the concerns raised by Bernard Williams and others about realism and moralism in political thought are not entirely new. Even if these questions have been raised in a more direct way, they do, nonetheless, refer back to a long history of political thinking. The dispute between realists and moralists is itself a reflection of value pluralism.

It is clear that a central feature of the debate about pluralism among political thinkers concerns reflection upon the nature and unavoidability of disagreement. It would be an obvious mistake to argue that all political disagreement has its source in pluralism. Nevertheless, it is the way in which plural values have the potential to be in conflict with each other that is the main reason why political theorists have found the topic interesting and challenging. In doing so, they are reminding themselves of one of the reasons why we have no option but to think about what – at the risk of pretentiousness – we can call, with Hannah Arendt or, more recently, with Pierre Manent's concepts of the 'human condition' in mind, 'the political condition' of humanity.[26]

Explicit consideration of the notion of the political condition, which is both central to and presupposed in all genuine political thinking, is surprisingly rare in modern political thought. The attention given to topics such as justice and rights far outweighs that given to the nature of politics itself.[27] If this tendency were to be reversed, political philosophical versions of applied ethics would not have such a central position. It would be more in keeping with the part of its history that accepted the existence of disagreement as its central problem and challenge. On the other hand, it is sometimes pointed out that there is a systematic bias in much of the history of political thought that sees endemic disagreement as a dangerous threat to stability. According to this interpretation, it understands itself as a consequence to be concerned, to a large degree with overcoming it. There are some important exceptions to this rule. One of the most significant and controversial is that offered by Hannah Arendt. Her interpretation of the history of political thought stressed the essential 'plurality' of the human world. In so doing, she struggled with the problem of what she saw as the inherent contradictions that reside in the concept and practice of political philosophy itself. In her view, the main tradition of political philosophy from Plato to Marx, in its desire to overcome both plurality and disagreement, suffers, paradoxically, from its own deeply anti-political character. However, Arendt's questionable distinction between 'the political' and 'the social' led her into some unnecessary conceptual difficulties. In addition, it is important to remember just how different Arendt's style of thinking is in its rejection of the idea of value pluralism, despite all of its talk of plurality. Arendt, in common with Leo Strauss, was unwilling or unable to recognize the point made by both Weber and Berlin 'that value conflict and moral disagreement are part of what constitutes us as both moderns and moral beings'.[28] But the main charge remains. Is the political tradition itself deeply anti-political? If it is, then we ought not to expect it to be able to say very much of interest about value pluralism or, in fact, about politics.

Whatever the merits of Arendt's overall case, it is clear that reflection upon value pluralism by political philosophers has not been as devoid of significance as her argument might lead us to expect. In particular, it is interesting to see how recourse to the example of Hume's account of the circumstances of justice has reappeared in discussions of the bases of disagreement and the need for politics. The significance and 'more disturbing possibility' of Hume's discussion lies in the suggestion that the 'deepest source of our moral disagreement in politics may reside in the human condition itself'.[29] Hume argued that moral conflicts that call for a just solution arise under the two conditions of moderate scarcity and the limits of human generosity. Hume argued that either a condition of abundance that satisfied our needs fully or the existence of extreme scarcity would eliminate moral and political conflict.

There is clearly an important insight here into the universality of the conditions that create disagreement and conflict. However, the modern recognition of value pluralism adds a new dimension. The problem is that one implication of value pluralism is that the fact of moral and political conflict is 'more deeply rooted in the human condition than the Humean circumstances of justice would have us believe'.[30] There is no reason to assume that conflict and disagreement will not continue under conditions of material abundance and unlimited generosity. In addition, there is the factor of incomplete understanding. Even if we had complete and perfect understanding, 'we do not know whether . . . we would discover uniquely correct resolutions to problems of incompatible values'.[31]

Recognition by political theorists of the centrality of the fact of disagreement as a significant aspect of pluralism has a habit of being both remembered and forgotten in turn. Nevertheless, the idea of the unavoidable reality of disagreement has been emphasized in an interesting way by Jeremy Waldron.[32] He argues strongly that our attitude to disagreement will, to a large degree, shape the way in which we think about politics. Further, he has pointed out that unless we take these 'elementary conditions' seriously 'nothing we say about politics makes much sense'. Adapting Rawls's Humean-inspired idea of 'the circumstances of justice', Waldron urges that we recognize the more fundamental 'circumstances of politics'. It is a strange fact that political theorists have not generally paid it much attention. 'The circumstances of politics' refers to 'the felt need among the members of a certain group for a common framework or decision or course of action on some matter, even in the face of disagreement about what that framework, decision or action should be'.[33]

In effect, Waldron accepts Rawls's 'burdens of judgement' argument, but takes it, he might say, to its logical conclusion. While Rawls uses this idea to make sense of disagreement between comprehensive philosophical doctrines, he wants to insulate our political arguments in order to make the search for stability feasible. Waldron points out that there is no convincing reason why the burdens of judgement, if we accept their significance, must not also apply to the world of political deliberation. Clearly, there is no reason to doubt that the:

circumstances under which people make judgements about issues like affirmative action, the legalization of abortion, the limits of free speech, the limits of the market, the proper extent of welfare provision, and the role of personal desert in economic justice are exactly those circumstances in which we would expect, given Rawls's account of the burdens of judgement, that reasonable people would differ.[34]

Just as scarcity and limited altruism are fundamental presuppositions for the circumstances of justice, so are disagreement and the need for common decision presupposed by the circumstances of politics. In other words, the question is not one of taking account of disagreement as such. Disagreement becomes a political problem in the light of the need for agreement as a basis for a collective decision. Waldron argues that:

> disagreement wouldn't matter if people didn't prefer a common decision; and the need for a common decision would not give rise to politics as we know it if there wasn't at least the potential for disagreement about what the common decision should be. On this account, imagining away the persistence of disagreement is like wishing away scarcity in an account of distributive justice.[35]

Waldron's emphasis upon disagreement is an important corrective of much that goes on in contemporary political theory. He points out that the attraction of elaborating models of democracy ought not to be allowed to get in the way of a more fundamental recognition of the fact that we live in a world of deep disagreement on moral and political questions. One of the merits of political liberalism is that it recognizes this and, to a large degree, can be regarded as an attempt to come to terms with the reality of disagreement and pluralism. However, as it has often been noted, modern political liberalism cannot easily accept the idea that disagreement can go all the way down, or, if not that far, at least as far as those things that it thinks that we must agree about. With political liberalism in mind, it is important to be clear that legislation takes place in the context of the circumstances of politics, and in particular of disagreement, and not:

in anything remotely resembling the justice-consensus that Rawlsians regard as essential to a well-ordered society. What is more, each of these legislative achievements claims authority and respect as law in the circumstances of politics, including the circumstances of disagreement as to whether it is even a step in the right direction. Such legislation does not claim authority and respect simply as an intimation of what an ideal society would be like; if it did, those with a different vision or social ideal would simply turn away.[36]

Waldron's answer to this problem is, at first glance, disarmingly direct. His response is to put his faith in legislation that has as its foundation the majority decisions of democratic assemblies. In addition, Waldron is committed to the principle that the legitimacy of political and legal institutions rests upon their justifiability to all those whose lives are affected by them. The idea of 'liberal legitimacy' has its roots in the Enlightenment ideal that 'everything real can in principle be justified, to everyone'. Modern political philosophy, in Waldron's account, is committed to the idea 'that theoretical argument aims not merely to justify laws or political proposals, but to justify them to the ordinary men and women whom they will affect'.[37] The question becomes one of how this is possible given the 'fact of disagreement' that Waldron takes as the basic political problem. If we accept the reality of the pervasiveness of reasonable disagreement, as Waldron argues that we must, it is hard to see how the legitimacy of majoritarian legislation is to be established.

Waldron is refreshingly straightforward about the possible challenges to his argument. Striking at the heart of his account is the charge that if we follow the logic of his position, then it would appear that, as he puts it, 'everything is up for grabs'. The argument that Waldron puts forward is, in part, conducted as a criticism of Ronald Dworkin's idea of the importance for democracy of judicial review. If we take the persistence of disagreement seriously, as Waldron contends, then even Dworkin's idea that we can use 'results-driven' criteria for constitutional design cannot succeed. If citizens disagree about what would count as the best or right results, then it is difficult to see how any form of constitutional design could be followed through and claim legitimacy. In Waldron's account, we are faced with a dilemma:

It looks as though it is disagreement all the way down, so far as constitutional choice is concerned. On the one hand, we cannot use a results-driven test, because we disagree about which results should count in favour of and which against a given decision-procedure. On the other hand, it seems we cannot appeal to any procedural criterion either, since procedural questions are at the very nub of the disagreements we are talking about.[38]

The fundamental and worrying charge that Waldron's theory, and any other theory for which the fact of disagreement is of central importance, faces is that it seems, despite itself, to have self-destructive implications. If we follow Waldron and argue that the correct response to the fact of disagreement is to be found in democratic majority rule, then, it also seems to follow, there appears to be no good reason to believe that the fact of disagreement will not apply to that too. Put differently, why ought we to expect agreement about the legitimacy of these democratic procedures? Waldron's own exposition is framed to a large degree in terms of an argument about the scope and nature of judicial review within democratic states.

The problems that arise from Waldron's work are instructive because they have broad implications for all those theoretical accounts that dwell upon the pervasive and persistent character of the reality of reasonable disagreement that is taken to be an unavoidable consequence of pluralism. A fundamental problem with this view is that Waldron is committed to two principles that lead to a deep contradiction. Waldron's criticism of the case for judicial review advanced by Dworkin is the outcome of his argument that the only acceptable form of political justification rests upon the procedures of majoritarian democracy. Anything that goes beyond this is bound to fail to attend to the deep and wide reality of reasonable disagreement that is to be expected in modern open societies and constitutional democracies.

There are negative and positive claims in Waldron's argument. The positive claim, which he calls 'fair proceduralism', is that 'political decisions can be rendered authoritative on the basis of their having been produced by a deliberative majoritarian process that is fair to all citizens and points of view'. The negative claim, which he calls 'deep disagreement', is that 'no position about what is required by fairness or justice or legitimacy is beyond reasonable disagreement'. The problem here is that these two claims cannot coexist within Waldron's liberal conception of political legitimacy. A 'reasonable objection' version of the criterion for legitimacy can be formulated. Here, 'political power is illegitimate unless there is a basis for it that is beyond reasonable objection'. However, if this is combined with the 'deep disagreement' thesis, the result seems to be philosophical anarchism: 'no claim to political authority is legitimate'. But philosophical anarchism is in contradiction with Waldron's own account of political legitimacy, based on the principle of 'fair proceduralism'.[39]

Estlund's response to Waldron's problem is to argue that he ought to drop one of the views to which he is committed. Given Waldron's defence of the 'no reasonable objection' view of political legitimacy, it appears that either the thesis of deep disagreement or the thesis of fair proceduralism will have to be abandoned. The proposal here is that the line that divides the reasonable from the unreasonable must be redrawn in order to limit the scope of disagreement. Estlund's criticism of Waldron raises a very difficult question for all theories that attempt to cope with and respect the significance of the depth of reasonable disagreement. The response would appear to be that, if we do not want to embrace a comprehensive form of political anarchism, then we have to accept the idea that disagreement over basic issues cannot always be assumed to be reasonable. Nor is it always as deep as Waldron and others who argue for the permanence and depth of disagreement say it is.

The significance of Waldron's work here is that he has faced the problem of disagreement directly. The main problem is that the strength of this analysis, stressing the centrality of disagreement for any theory of politics, is also liable, at the same time, to be its main weakness. If reasonable disagreement gives way to deep disagreement which goes all the way down, then it is difficult to see how any kind of political legitimacy based upon liberal principles can work; nor is it clear how any such political theory can be other than self-defeating.

One of the implications of Waldron's account of the fact of disagreement is to put a brake upon the claims of the more enthusiastic proponents of the theory of deliberative democracy. Although we ought not to discount the importance of deliberation, Waldron is right to point out that we are just as likely to disagree after deliberating as we were before doing so. The basic, and correct, idea is that the 'prospect of persisting disagreement must be regarded . . . as one of the elementary conditions of modern politics. Nothing we say about politics makes sense if we proceed without taking this condition into account.'[40]

Discussions of pluralism would seem to possess a natural affinity with the idea of democracy. It is not too much of an exaggeration to say that, more than any other political arrangement, democracy is generally thought to be the most open to the fact of pluralism. Certainly, for many of the hostile critics of democracy throughout the history of western political thought, its supposed contribution to the persistence of pluralism and disagreement was taken to be one of the main reasons why it was so discredited. Nevertheless, a curious feature of much contemporary debate about democracy has been the way in which it has been enlisted as a response to pluralism once its deliberative aspects have been defined as its most important feature. However, this idea of a natural affinity between pluralism and democracy has not gone unchallenged. Galston, for example, has argued forcefully that:

> if there are good reasons to take value pluralism seriously . . . , then it becomes impossible to accord democracy normative authority over all other claims, public and nonpublic. Not only is the scope of democratic political authority restricted; certain alternatives to democracy within the sphere of politics must be taken more seriously than they usually are.[41]

In the debate among political theorists concerning the correct response to the problem of pluralism, the idea of deliberative democracy has begun to occupy a prominent position. The concept of deliberative democracy at first seems to be a pleonasm. After all, how can democracy not be deliberative, or at least not imply a degree of deliberation, in some sense? However, the proponents of deliberative democracy obviously mean something more specific in their use of the term. Not surprisingly, perhaps, the concept has been used in different ways. The simple question here is this: is some form of deliberative democracy the best response to the reality of value pluralism and the persistence of disagreement that is available to us (in relatively liberal constitutional states)?

Their bias towards the search for agreement leads deliberative democrats to think that disagreement is a sign of perceived
failure or incompleteness.[42] In addition, the idea of deliberative
democracy sometimes seems to be favoured as an alternative
form of radical theory to fill the vacuum on the left created by
the decline in the theory and practice of Marxian socialism.
However, in response, it is worth repeating Michael Walzer's
question: 'Deliberation, and What Else?' It is not necessary,
Walzer points out, to sign up to Carl Schmitt's vision of politics
in order to recognize the persistence of disagreement in politics
and the way in which different interests, values and ideologies
are often irreconcilable. Political conflict between right and
left in western states remains a persistent and deeply embedded fact of public life. Politics is, and will remain to a large
degree, 'the endless return of these disagreements and conflicts, the struggle to manage and contain them, and, at the
same time, to win whatever temporary victories are available'.
There is no way in which deliberation, however perfect and
democratic, can avoid or resolve these basic features of the
political condition.[43]

The idea of democratic deliberation is often defended on
epistemic grounds. Democracy is defended as a method for
resolving disagreements that are founded upon differences in
basic value commitments. This can be understood as an argument to the effect that the virtue of democracy in general and
of deliberative democracy in particular rests on the idea that
it ought to be thought of as a truth-seeking practice. This view
can lend itself to a defence framed in pragmatist terms.[44] The
pragmatic approach is important because it accepts the idea
that 'the multiplicity of values which are carried to moral
deliberation is a modern phenomenon, perhaps the defining
feature of modernity'.[45] However, according to some pragmatists, the pluralism of values need not be the cause of too much
distress. The fact of pluralism does not mean that we cannot
aim for truth and reasonableness in our beliefs.

The pragmatist defence of democracy is particularly interesting because it accepts that pluralism and disagreement are
genuine problems for moral and political theory. However, the
pragmatist response is to steer a course between the scepticism, on the one hand, about the relevance of liberal and
democratic ideas advanced most dramatically, for instance, by

Carl Schmitt and some of his latter-day followers, and, on the other hand, the strong programme of justification proposed, most importantly, for example, by Jürgen Habermas and Karl Otto Apel. In the face of this dichotomy, a common response of political theorists has been to establish some set of objective universal standards that promise to provide an external standpoint for settling value conflicts. Unfortunately, this never seems to be entirely convincing because, on close inspection, the proposed standards prove to be not really universal or relevant to the appropriate situations.[46]

An interesting aspect of the pragmatist case is advanced by Misak's discussion of the threat posed to the liberal and democratic responses to pluralism due to strong versions of scepticism about the place of reason in politics. In modern discussions, this is most frequently identified with the ideas of Carl Schmitt. Schmitt's significance in the history of modern political thought rests to a large degree upon his controversial claims about what he considered to be the true nature of 'the political'. As far as the questions of value pluralism and political disagreement are concerned, Schmitt denied the possibility of any convincing or persuasive appeals to the rational or the reasonable as a way for settling political conflicts. It is here we can see that the debate about the significance of value pluralism opens up a very deep divide in the history of modern political thought. Is there something in the nature of politics that is resistant, at the deepest level, to the operation of reason?

Even if we do not agree that the sheer diversity of values that shape moral and political deliberation is a defining characteristic of modernity, it is hard to deny that it must have some significance. At the same time, it is unnecessary to assume that the lack of belief in the availability of a foundational set of principles, that is the presumed effect of disenchantment, need necessarily give rise to the degree of existential gloom that some theorist find, and to a degree endorse, for example, in the thought of political thinkers such as Max Weber.[47]

Arguing from a pragmatist standpoint, Misak suggests that the best response to anxieties about the place of reason in ethics and politics brought about by the recognition of pluralism is to think of political argument and disagreement in terms of a search for true and reasonable beliefs. Nevertheless, it has to be admitted that the prospects for the implied convergence in political beliefs are not promising. Furthermore, as Misak admits, this would not be a desirable outcome, as disagreement and opposition are normally taken to be signs of health in democracies. In fact, as has often been noted, the practice of deliberation is unlikely to generate agreement rather than disagreement.[48] Despite their ingenuity, theories of this kind are unable to dispel the worry that they deliver a method that 'leaves little room for whatever is distinctive of morals or political discourse'.[49]

The discussion about value pluralism has focused on two major themes in the response of political theorists. One is exemplified by Rawls whose basic intention is to strive for reconciliation. It is this commitment that gives substance to his more explicit concern with the problem of political stability. Rawls wants 'to ask whether the fact of reasonable pluralism is a historical fact we should lament'.[50] The aim of his 'realistically utopian' theory is to show that the existence of value pluralism is not necessarily a bad thing and that, in fact, it has considerable benefits. Indeed it seems that the advent of modern pluralism is more than just one historical possibility among others, but can be considered to be a more providential opportunity to exercise our higher moral powers.[51] Acceptance of his theory, Rawls argues, will reconcile us 'in part' to our condition.

The idea that the aim of a theory ought to be reconciliation is also bound up with a conception of the nature of the 'ideal' nature of political theory. The reduction or eradication of disagreement and conflict between ideals and values is both a reason for and a consequence of this commitment. There is an implicit assumption here that is not remarked upon often enough. This is the idea that a situation where there is little or no conflict or disagreement is better than one in which there is. The reduction of conflict or disagreement is taken to be the main aim for both political theory and practice.[52] In Rawls's case, these ideas are bound up, most clearly in his earlier work, with a particular view of the need for a more systematic and unified moral theory whose structure and purpose would be comparable in some ways to linguistic or logical theory. Such a theory would, it is argued, serve to 'order our thoughts' and 'reduce disagreements' and 'bring divergent convictions more in line'.[53] This continued to be a guiding thread in Rawls's thought throughout all its later changes and developments.

Whether or not this is the right procedure for moral theory, it is not at all obvious that it is the best way to think about politics. Even if there is a need for consistency in the making of public decisions, party programmes and policies, this does not automatically apply to the entire political domain. Where conflicts and disagreements about values and the interpretation of values are of central importance, as they are in the most important areas of political life, then it ought not to be assumed too readily that the job of the theorist is to find agreement, compromise or reconciliation. Why be reconciled with a world that is abhorrent or deeply flawed?

There is another view of political theory that is more attuned to the pervasive and persistent character of disagreement and conflict as constitutive features of the political domain. Rather than seek the grounds for agreement, compromise or reconciliation, the thought here is that clarifying as much as possible the nature and implications of the values to which we are committed can sharpen rather than reduce our differences and disagreements. Max Weber presents us with a clear example of this standpoint. Assuming the existence of the 'eternal conflict' between ethical theories and the political standpoints to which they are often related, Weber argued that it is the task of the theorist to engage in a discussion of those values in order to clarify their inner structure and possible implications. However, such a discussion is just as likely to highlight their incommensurability and differences as it is to demonstrate their supposed deeper levels of agreement. There is no compelling reason to believe that a compromise between, to take Weber's example, the radically opposed views of a revolutionary anarcho-syndicalist and a conservative 'Realpolitiker' over the question of political ethics and practice is closer to the truth. Indeed, Weber is right to point out that a debate of this kind between radically opposed views can make a significant contribution to the important task of self-clarification. Through a confrontation with our opponent's commitments, we come to a better understanding of our own values as well as those of our opponent.

The tension between these two ideas of the nature and purpose of political theory, of reconciliation and separation, might itself be a reflection of a deeper tension that is embedded in the western idea of politics. Of course, the proponent of the idea of reconciliation expressed, for example, in various forms of normative ideal theory could also claim that those who focus upon and seek to sharpen disagreement do not have a monopoly upon conceptual clarification. This is true. The point, however, is that pre-judgement of the need for reconciliation will deaden the senses to those features that are specific for the political domain.

According to some of its critics, much of modern political theory is guilty of accepting the reality of pluralism and disagreement, but at the cost of seriously underestimating the scope and depth of its implications. This criticism, in its extreme form, argues that all normative theory has become infected by the liberal virus. It is claimed that the problem is not simply one of the narrow scope of a theory that can be rectified, but that 'liberalism actually misunderstands the nature of politics, and as a result seeks to displace real politics altogether'.[54] There is a deep disagreement between those theorists who would make the fact of disagreement central to their view of politics and those who, while not denying its existence, do not want to accept what are claimed to be its negative implications for liberal or any normative theory.

There are several versions of the critical view of liberal theory that, despite their differences, rely upon the idea that endemic disagreement is one of the most important and unavoidable features of the political domain. There are various background influences at work. Generally speaking, the idea seems to be that a more descriptive rather than normative account of the political world would redress the balance. Political thinkers such as Hobbes and Machiavelli who were concerned with contingency and power are pointed to as examples of the kind of political thinking that we need, rather than that of, for example, Kant or Rawls.

One influential version of this charge draws for its inspiration upon the political thought of Carl Schmitt. However, the use of Schmitt here is highly selective, and is most useful if used in this way and 'thinks with Schmitt against Schmitt'.[55] Schmitt is often taken as a reference point or as an authority for a view of politics that serves as a necessary corrective to the dominant liberal view in Anglo-American political philosophy. Although Schmitt regarded 'the political' as a domain of unavoidable conflict between 'friend' and 'enemy', and was opposed to parliamentary democracy, his views have been adapted to be more in keeping with the requirements of modern states. In order to construct an account of 'agonistic democracy', the opposition between 'friend' and 'enemy' has been softened so that 'the enemy' becomes an 'adversary' who must be tolerated and struggled against within the political community, but is not to be destroyed as in Schmitt's example. The category of 'the enemy' remains nevertheless as a description for those who refuse to accept the rules of the democratic game. The explicit intention here, it must be added, is to strengthen liberal democracy rather than to destroy it.

Although it is clear that acknowledging the centrality of endemic disagreement does not fatally undermine the case for liberal or normative theory, it does point to some of the limitations of this genre. As one of the defenders of liberal and normative theory admits, the correct view is probably somewhere between the extremes. It is misleading to claim that those who stress the persistence of endemic disagreement are also claiming that disagreement about everything is endemic.[56] It is enough to recognize that although disagreement is not a uniquely political problem, it does present politics with its own distinct range of problems. It is not necessary to agree with a conception of the autonomy of the political derived from the work of Carl Schmitt to see that applied moral philosophy does not constitute the whole of political philosophy.[57] Trying to understand political reality is no less important than arriving at normative recommendations. Indeed, the latter ought to presuppose the former. If the reality and persistence of disagreement is central for our understanding of politics, it is important to recognize that if political disagreement might involve moral disagreement it does not follow that all political disagreement can be accurately described as being no more than moral disagreement concerning political questions.

The response to pluralism in modern political thought has moved backwards and forwards between the kind of existentialist view put forward, for example, by Max Weber in some of his moods and the attempt to contain it on the basis of an appeal to shared beliefs. It seems that if modern political thought is caught in the pluralist predicament, then accepting the 'existential' element in pluralism is to deny the possibility of any kind of detached theorizing that can rise above the 'war of the gods'. The voice of the theorist is not only that of a spectator but also that of a participant. Perhaps all political theorists can be described in anthropological terms as participant observers. Their fieldwork is simply to live in and reflect upon the political conflicts and problems of their time.[58]

Clearly, recognition of the centrality of pluralism and disagreement in the modern political order raises the question of the role and authority of the political theorist. If we take pluralism and disagreement seriously, what are the implications for our understanding of the nature of political theory? Jeremy Waldron is right to point out that the way in which we answer these questions has deep implications for our view of the distinctive character and limits of political philosophy. Political theorists such as John Rawls are not simply looking at disagreements about justice as detached spectators. In putting forward their theories, they are also engaged in these disagreements as participants. After all, that is why they think that these disputes are important in the first place. Recognition that the theorist's detachment from the realities of the polis can never be total is not an entirely new idea. After all, to put it plainly, modern political philosophy in the 'normative philosophy-and-public-affairs-mode is simply conscientious civic discourse'.[59] Whether this is a distinctively modern notion that is intrinsically connected to the recognition of pluralism is an open question. Thomas Hobbes is one example of a theorist who was self-conscious about his role as both spectator and participant in political controversies. In *Leviathan*, a work addressed to the problem of political disagreement, Hobbes, after distancing his work from Plato's *Republic*, and implying that there is no escape from the cave, states that the most that he can hope for is that 'this writing of mine may fall into the hands of a sovereign who will consider it himself . . . [and] . . . convert this truth of speculation into the utility of practice'.[60] Perhaps one role of the political philosopher is to be the destroyer of illusions rather than the provider of the wished for but illusive foundations for particular practices.[61] In conclusion, we can say that the debates about pluralism in modern political philosophy have had at least one positive outcome. They have forced us to think about some of the most basic questions about the nature of politics and our reflections upon it.

Notes and References

Chapter 1   Pluralism

1   Bernard Williams, 'Relativism, History, and the Existence of Values', in Joseph Raz, *The Practice of Value*. Oxford: Crandon Press, 2003, p. 117.
2   Richard E. Flathman, *Pluralism and Liberal Democracy*. Baltimore, NJ: Johns Hopkins Press, 2005, p. 1.
3   Mason, Elinor, 'Value Pluralism', *Stanford Encyclopaedia of Philosophy* (fall 2008 edn), ed. Edward N. Zalta. Available at: <http://plato.stanford.edu/archives/fall2008/ entries/value-pluralism/>.
4   Ronald Beiner, 'The Moral Vocabulary of Monism', in *Nomos* 34: *Virtue*, ed. John W. Chapman and William A. Galston. New York: New York University Press, 1992, pp. 145–84.
5   For example, Charles Taylor, 'Leading a Life', in Ruth Chang (ed.), *Incommensurability, Incomparability, and Practical Reason*. Cambridge, MA: Harvard University Press, 1997, pp. 170–83.
6   Charles Larmore, 'The Limits of Aristotelian Ethics', *Nomos* 34: *Virtue*, pp. 185–203.
7   Friedrich Nietzsche, *Beyond Good and Evil*. London: Penguin, 1973, p. 16.
8   See Herbert Schnädelbach, *Philosophy in Germany 1831–1933*. Cambridge: Cambridge University Press, 1984, pp. 161–91.
9   Carl Schmitt, *The Tyranny of Values*. Washington, DC: Plutarch Press, 1996.
10   Hannah Arendt, *The Human Condition*. Chicago, IL: University of Chicago Press, 1958.

11 John Skorupski, 'Value-Pluralism', in David Archard (ed.), *Philosophy and Pluralism*. Cambridge: Cambridge University Press, 1996, p. 101.

12 Robert B. Talisse, 'Can Value Pluralists be Comprehensive Liberals? Galston's *Liberal Pluralism*', *Contemporary Political Theory* (2004) 3: 128–9.

13 Ruth Chang, 'Value Pluralism', *International Encyclopaedia of Social and Behavioural Science*, vol. 24, ed. Neil J. Smelser and Paul B. Baltes. Amsterdam: Elsevier, 2001, pp. 16139–45.

14 Isaiah Berlin, *Four Essays on Liberty*. Oxford: Oxford University Press, 1969, pp. 200–1.

15 William A. Galston, *Liberal Pluralism*. Cambridge: Cambridge University Press, 2002, p. 5.

16 Isaiah Berlin, *Liberty*. Oxford: Oxford University Press, 2002, pp. 212–17.

17 John Rawls, 'The Domain of the Political and Overlapping Consensus', *Collected Papers*, ed. Samuel Freeman. Cambridge, MA: Harvard University Press, 1999, pp. 473–96.

18 John Rawls, *Collected Papers*, p. 462.

19 W. A. Galston, *Liberal Pluralism*, pp. 5–6.

20 Bernard Williams, *Moral Luck*. Cambridge, MA: Cambridge University Press, 1981, p. 72.

21 Ibid., p. 80.

22 See, for example, Glen Newey, *After Politics*. London: Palgrave, 2001.

23 Jeremy Waldron, *Law and Disagreement*. Oxford: Oxford University Press, 1999, pp. 105–6.

24 See Larry Krasnoff, 'The Fact of Politics: History and Teleology in Kant', *European Journal of Philosophy* 1/1 (1993): 22–40; Raymond Geuss, *Outside Ethics*. Princeton, NJ: Princeton University Press, 2005, pp. 11–28; Jeremy Waldron, *The Dignity of Legislation*. Cambridge: Cambridge University Press, 1999, pp. 153–6.

25 On the centrality of disagreement in Greek moral and political thought, see Nicholas White, *Individual and Conflict in Greek Ethics*. Oxford: Clarendon Press, 2002.

26 Jeremy Waldron, *Law and Disagreement*, pp. 1–17.

27 For an overview, see Samantha Besson, *The Morality of Conflict*, Oxford and Portland, OR: Hart Publishing, 2005, p. 1.

28 Charles Larmore, *The Morals of Modernity*. Cambridge: Cambridge University Press, 1996, p. 168.

29 Alasdair MacIntyre, *After Virtue*. Notre Dame, IN: University of Notre Dame Press, 1981, p. 6.

30 J. Griffin, 'Incommensurability: What's the Problem?', in R. Chang (ed.), *Incommensurability, Incomparability, and Practical Reason.* pp. 35–51.

31 Charles Larmore, *The Morals of Modernity*, p. 152.

32 Ibid., p. 167.

33 Charles Taylor, *Sources of the Self.* Cambridge: Cambridge University Press, 1989, p. 18.

34 Susan Mendus, 'Pluralism and Scepticism in a Disenchanted World', in Maria Baghramian and Attracta Ingram (eds), *Pluralism: The Philosophy and Politics of Diversity.* London and New York: Routledge, 2000, p. 106.

35 See, for example, Sylvie Mesure and Alain Renaut, *La guerre des dieux.* Paris: Bernard Grasset, 1996.

36 Henry S. Richardson, *Practical Reasoning about Final Ends.* Cambridge: Cambridge University Press, Cambridge, 1997, p. 237.

37 Ibid., p. 238.

38 Steven Lukes, *Liberals and Cannibals.* London: Verso, 2003, pp. 63–77.

39 Geuss, *Outside Ethics*, pp. 155–6.

40 Gerald F. Gaus, *Contemporary Theories of Liberalism.* London: Sage, 2003, pp. 13–14.

41 Ibid., p. 231.

42 Stuart Hampshire, *Justice is Conflict.* Princeton, NJ: Princeton University Press, 2000, p. 33.

43 Bernard Williams, *In the Beginning was the Deed.* Princeton, NJ: Princeton University Press, 2005, p. 13.

44 A typical example example is Chantal Mouffe, *The Return of the Political.* London: Verso, 1993.

45 Aurel Kolnai, 'The Moral Theme in Political Division', *Philosophy* 35 (1960): 234.

46 Bernard Williams, *In the Beginning was the Deed*, p. 52.

47 W. B. Gallie, *Philosophy and the Historical Understanding.* London: Chatto and Windus, 1964, pp. 157–91.

48 Gerald F. Gaus, *Political Concepts and Political Theories.* Boulder, CO, and Oxford: Westview Press, 2000.

49 Bernard Yack, 'Putting Injustice First: An Alternative Approach to Liberal Pluralism', *Social Research* 66/4 (1999): 1103.

50 Ibid.

51 Raymond Geuss, *Outside Ethics*, pp. 17–19.

52 I am paraphrasing the remarks of David Wiggins in his *Needs, Values, Truth.* Oxford: Clarendon Press, 2002, p. 316.

53 Raymond Geuss, *Outside Ethics*, p. 31.

54 Raymond Geuss, 'Politics and Morals', *RSA Journal* (September 2008); *Politics and the Imagination*. Princeton, NJ: Princeton University Press, 2009, p. 40.
55 Stuart Hampshire, *Justice is Conflict*, p. 34.
56 I have taken this term from Pierre Manent, *A World beyond Politics?* Princeton, NJ: Princeton University Press, 2006.

Chapter 2 Pluralism and Pessimism

1 John Rawls, *Collected Papers*, pp. 462–3. This footnote occurs in a modified form in the version of this paper, 'Priority of Right and Ideas of the Good', that appears in Rawls's *Political Liberalism*. New York: Columbia University Press, 1996, p. 197. The reference to Weber is omitted here.
2 John Rawls, *Justice as Fairness: A Restatement*. Cambridge, MA: Harvard University Press, 2001, pp. 154–5.
3 Max Weber, *The Methodology of the Social Sciences*. New York: The Free Press, 1949, p. 14.
4 *Max Weber's 'Science as a Vocation'*, ed. Peter Lassman and Irving Velody. London: Unwin Hyman, 1989, pp. 22–3.
5 Max Weber, *The Methodology of the Social Sciences*, p. 60.
6 Max Kölbel, 'Faultless Disagreement', *Proceedings of the Aristotelian Society*, 2003, pp. 53–73.
7 Max Weber, *The Methodology of the Social Sciences*, p. 16.
8 Ibid., p. 57.
9 'Weber: Political Writings', ed. Peter Lassman and Ronald Speirs. Cambridge: Cambridge University Press, 1994, pp. 357–69.
10 Bernard Williams, *Moral Luck*, p. 72.
11 Ibid., p. 222.
12 *Max Weber's 'Science as a Vocation'*, ed. Peter Lassman and Irving Velody, pp. 15–16.
13 Steven Lukes, *Liberals and Cannibals*, pp. 63–77.
14 Hilary Putnam, *Reason, Truth, and History*. Cambridge: Cambridge University Press, 1981, p. 174.
15 Ibid., p. 177.
16 Max Weber, *The Methodology of the Social Sciences*, pp. 12–13.
17 For example, in John Rawls's idea of 'the burdens of judgement' and, in a different way, Paul Ricoeur, 'The Political Paradox', in W. Connolly, ed., *Legitimacy and the State*. Oxford: Blackwell, 1984, pp. 250–72; first published in Paul Ricoeur, *History and Truth*, Evanston, IL: Northwestern University Press, 1965.
18 Wilhelm Hennis, *Max Weber: Essays in Reconstruction*. London: Allen and Unwin, 1988, p. 158.

19 Friedrich Nietzsche, *The Gay Science*. New York: Vintage, 1974, p. 279.
20 H. Gildin (ed.), *Political Philosophy: Six Essays by Leo Strauss*. New York: Bobbs Merrill, 1975, p. 95.
21 This is a basic theme in Hannah Arendt's work.
22 *Max Weber's 'Science as a Vocation'*, ed. Peter Lassman and Irving Velody, p. 26.
23 Ibid., p. 154.
24 Dirk Käsler, 'Max Weber', in I. Fetscher and H. Munkler (eds), *Pipers Handbuch der Politischen Ideen*. Munich: Piper, 1987, p. 156.
25 This was the famous charge made by Habermas, but later significantly modified. See O. Stammer (ed.), *Max Weber and Sociology Today*. Oxford: Blackwell, 1971, p. 66.
26 Charles Taylor, 'Plurality of Goods', in Ronald Dworkin et al. (eds), *The Legacy of Isaiah Berlin. New York Review of Books*, 2001, p. 117.
27 Ernest Gellner, 'Sauce for the Liberal Goose, *Prospect* (November 1995): 58.
28 Ibid., p. 58.
29 Ira Katznelson, 'Isaiah Berlin's Modernity', *Social Research* 66 (1999): 4.
30 Bernard Williams, *Moral Luck*, p. 71.
31 Isaiah Berlin, *Concepts and Categories*. Oxford: Oxford University Press, 1980, p. 149.
32 Isaiah Berlin, *The Hedgehog and the Fox: An Essay on Tolstoy's View of History*. London: Weidenfeld and Nicolson, 1953, p. 1.
33 Ramin Jahanbegloo, *Conversations with Isaiah Berlin*. London: Phoenix, 1992, p. 46.
34 Isaiah Berlin, *The Crooked Timber of Humanity*. London: Fontana, 1991, pp. 5–6.
35 Ibid., p. 13.
36 Ruth Chang (ed.), *Incommensurability, Incomparability, and Practical Reason*.
37 'Isaiah Berlin in Conversation with Steven Lukes', *Salmagundi* 120 (1998): 101–3.
38 Isaiah Berlin, 'Rationality of Value Judgements', in C. J. Friedrich (ed.), *Rational Decision, Nomos 7*. New York: Atherton Press, 1964, pp. 221–3.
39 Leo Strauss, 'Relativism', in H. Schoeck (ed.), *Relativism and the Study of Man*. Princeton, NJ: Van Nostrand, 1961, p. 140.
40 Isaiah Berlin, *Four Essays on Liberty*, p. 165.
41 Leo Strauss, 'Relativism', p. 138.

42   Michael Sandel (ed.), *Liberalism and its Critics*. Oxford: Blackwell, 1984, p. 8.
43   Isaiah Berlin, *Four Essays*, p. 172.
44   Michael Sandel, *Liberalism and its Critics*, p
45   Richard Rorty, *Contingency, Irony, and Solidarity*. Cambridge: Cambridge University Press, 1989, p. 53.
46   John Gray, *Berlin*. London: Fontana, 1995.
47   Ramin Jahanbegloo, *Conversations with Isaiah Berlin*, p 32.
48   Isaiah Berlin, 'The Alleged Relativism in Eighteenth-Century Thought', in Berlin, *The Crooked Timber*. Berlin is responding to Arnaldo Momigliani, 'On the Pioneer Trail', *New York Review of Books*, 11 November 1976, pp. 33–8.
49   Isaiah Berlin, *The Crooked Timber*, p. 80.
50   Ibid., p. 11.
51   Ibid., p. 79.
52   Isaiah Berlin, *The Sense of Reality*. London: Pimlico, 1996, pp. 168–93.
53   Ibid., p. 170.
54   Ibid., pp. 191–2.
55   Mark Lilla, 'The Trouble with the Enlightenment', *London Review of Books*, 6 January 1994, pp. 12–13.
56   Isaiah Berlin, *The Crooked Timber*, p. 13.
57   Ibid., p. 11.
58   Richard Wollheim, 'The Idea of a Common Human Nature', in Edna Ullmann-Margalit and Avishai Margalit (eds), *Isaiah Berlin: A Celebration*. Chicago, IL: University of Chicago Press, 1991, p. 65.
59   Isaiah Berlin, *Concepts and Categories*, p. 164.
60   Perry Anderson, *A Zone of Engagement*. London: Verso, 1992), p. 244.
61   Isaiah Berlin, *Concepts and Categories*, p. 166.
62   Isaiah Berlin, *The Crooked Timber*, p. 17.
63   Isaiah Berlin, *Four Essays*, pp. 171–2.
64   Isaiah Berlin, *The Crooked Timber*, p. 17.
65   'Isaiah Berlin in Conversation with Steven Lukes', *Salmagundi* 120 (fall 1998): 52–134.
66   Isaiah Berlin, *The Sense of Reality*, pp. 168–93.
67   Ramin Jahanbegloo, *Conversations with Isaiah Berlin*, p. 44.
68   Steven Lukes, 'The Singular and the Plural: On the Distinctive Liberalism of Isaiah Berlin', *Social Research* 61/3 (1994): 687–717.
69   Steven Lukes, 'An Unfashionable Fox', in Ronald Dworkin et al. (eds), *The Legacy of Isaiah Berlin*. New York: New York Review of Books, 2001, pp. 43–57.
70   Ian Shapiro, 'Gross Concepts in Political Argument', *Political Theory* 17/ 1 (1989): 51–76.

71   Michael Walzer, 'Are there Limits to Liberalism?', *New York Review of Books* (19 October 1995), p. 29.
72   Isaiah Berlin and Bernard Williams, 'Pluralism and Liberalism: A Reply', *Political Studies* 42 (1994): 306–9. This is a reply to George Crowder, 'Pluralism and Liberalism', *Political Studies* 42 (1994): 293–305.
73   Charles Larmore, *The Morals of Modernity*, p. 151.
74   Isaiah Berlin, *Four Essays on Liberty*, p. 167.
75   Ibid., pp. 168–9.
76   Noel O'Sullivan, 'Visions of Freedom: The Response to Totalitarianism', in J. Hayward, B. Barry, A.Brown (eds), *The British Study of Politics in the Twentieth Century*. Oxford: Oxford University Press, 1999, pp. 63–88.
77   On Popper's recognition of value pluralism, see his *Unended Quest*. London: Fontana, 1976, p. 116.
78   See the discussion in Ronald Dworkin et al. (eds), *The Legacy of Isaiah Berlin*, pp 59–69.
79   'Isaiah Berlin in Conversation with Steven Lukes', *Salmagundi* 120 (1998): 102.
80   Isaiah Berlin, *Liberty*, p. 48.
81   'Isaiah Berlin in Conversation with Steven Lukes', p. 96. It also ought to be mentioned that Berlin does elsewhere recognize that 'the founders of modern sociology' – Marx, Weber, Durkheim – were not guilty of arguing for a doctrine of historical inevitability. See Berlin, *Liberty*, p. 158.
82   See, for example, Raymond Aron, 'Max Weber and Modern Social Science', in F. Draws (ed.), *History, Truth, Liberty*. Chicago, IL: University of Chicago Press, 1985, pp. 335–73.
83   John Gray, *Berlin*, p. 58.
84   Ernest Gellner, 'Sauce for the Liberal Goose', *Prospect* (November 1995): 58.
85   Leo Strauss, *Natural Right and History*. Chicago, IL: University of Chicago Press, 1950, pp 35–80.
86   Ibid., p. 36.
87   Ibid., p. 64.
88   Ibid., p. 65.
89   Wilhelm Hennis has put forward a response to Strauss that attempts to resituate Weber within the classical tradition of political thought. See Hennis, *Max Weber: Essays in Reconstruction*, p. 91.
90   Ramin Jahanbegloo, *Conversations with Isaiah Berlin*, p. 32.
91   T. L. Pangle, *The Rebirth of Classical Rationalism*, ed. Leo Strauss. Chicago, IL: University of Chicago Press, 1989, p. 16.
92   David Dyzenhaus, *Legality and Legitimacy*. Oxford: Clarendon Press, 1997; Peter Lassman, 'Disenchantment and the Liberalism

of Fear', in Mark Evans (ed.), *The Edinburgh Companion to Contemporary Liberalism*. Edinburgh: Edinburgh University Press, 2001, pp. 135–47.

93   Isaiah Berlin, *Concepts and Categories*, p. 166.

94   Isaiah Berlin, *The Crooked Timber of Humanity*, p. 203.

95   Isaiah Berlin, 'Rationality of Value Judgments', in Friedrich (ed.), *Rational Decision, Nomos 7*, pp. 221–3.

96   Michael Sandel, *Liberalism and its Critics*, p. 8.

97   In particular, see Sterling P. Lamprecht, 'The Need for a Pluralistic Emphasis in Ethics', *The Journal of Philosophy, Psychology and Scientific Methods* 17/21 (1920): 561–72, and also his 'Some Political Implications of 'Ethical Pluralism' in the same journal, 17/9 (1921): 225–44.

98   Perry Anderson, *A Zone of Engagement*, p. 243.

99   For example, Ronald Dworkin et al. (eds), *The Legacy of Isaiah Berlin*.

100 Richard E. Flathman, *Pluralism and Liberal Democracy*, p. 76.

101 Stuart Hampshire, *Justice is Conflict*, p. 43.

102 Ibid., p. 77.

103 Ibid., pp. 117–18.

104 Stuart Hampshire, *Morality and Conflict*. Cambridge, MA: Harvard University Press, 1983, p. 151.

105 Stuart Hampshire, *Innocence and Experience*, London: Allen Lane, Penguin, 1989 pp. 51–2.

106 Ibid., p. 113.

107 Stuart Hampshire, *Justice is Conflict*, p. 34.

108 Stuart Hampshire, *Innocence and Experience*, p. 119.

109 Stuart Hampshire, 'Uncertainty in Politics', *Encounter* (1957).

110 Stuart Hampshire, *Innocence and Experience*, p. 137.

111 Ibid.,, pp. 141–2.

112 Stuart Hampshire, *Justice as Conflict*, p xi. Hampshire's views can be compared with the 'Liberalism of Fear' outlined by Judith Shklar.

113 Stuart Hampshire, *Justice is Conflict*, p xii.

114 Ibid., p. 43.

115 Joshua Cohen, 'Pluralism and Proceduralism', *Chicago-Kent Law Review* 69 (1994): 589–618.

116 Ibid., p. 593.

117 Ibid., p. 594.

118 Stuart Hampshire, *Justice is Conflict*, p. 39.

119 Ibid., p. 97.

120 John Gray, *Berlin*, p. 1.

121 For example, *Heresies: Against Progress and other Illusions*. London: Granta, 2004, and *Straw Dogs: Thoughts on Humans and other Animals*. London: Granta, 2003.

122 He calls Nietzsche 'late modern Europe's greatest Enlightenment thinker' in his *Voltaire*. London: Phoenix, 1998, p. 52.

123 See, for example, James Schmidt, 'Civility, Enlightenment, and Society: Conceptual Confusions and Kantian Remedies', *American Political Science Review* 92/2 (1998): 419–27.

124 James Schmidt, 'What Enlightenment Project?', *Political Theory* 28/6 (2000): 734–57; Bernard Yack, *The Fetishism of Modernities*. Notre Dame: University of Notre Dame, 1997.

125 John Gray, 'After the New Liberalism', *Social Research* 61/3 (1994): 721; reprinted in Gray, *Enlightenment's Wake*. London: Routledge, 1995.

126 See Mark Lilla, 'What is Counter-Enlightenment?', in J. Mali and R. Wokler (eds), *Isaiah Berlin's Counter-Enlightenment*. Philadelphia: American Philosophical Society, 2003, pp. 1–11.

127 Gray does elsewhere present a more nuanced view. He refers to the Enlightenment as 'an extended family of intellectual and political movements' in his *Voltaire*, p. 3.

128 John Gray, *Two Faces of Liberalism*. Cambridge: Polity, 2000, p. 138.

129 See Gerald F. Gaus, *Contemporary Theories of Liberalism*.

130 John Gray, *Berlin*, p. 142.

131 Ibid., p. 143.

132 Bernard Williams, 'Introduction' to Isaiah Berlin, *Concepts and Categories*.

133 John Gray, *Berlin*, p. 145.

134 Michael Walzer, 'Are there Limits to Liberalism?', *New York Review of Books, Books* (19 October 1995), p. 29.

135 John Gray, *Post-Liberalism: Studies in Political Thought*. London: Routledge, 1993, pp. 64–5.

136 Ibid., p. 65.

137 John Gray, *Berlin*, p. 155.

138 Alan Ryan, 'Live and Let Live', *New York Review of Books*, 48/8 (2001), available at: <http://www.nybooks.com/articles/archives/2001/may/17/live-and-let-live/>.

139 John Gray, *Two Faces of Liberalism*, p. 105.

140 Gerald F. Gaus, *Contemporary Theories of Liberalism*, p. 49.

141 John Gray, *Two Faces of Liberalism*, p. 33.

142 Robert B. Talisse, 'Two Faced Liberalism', *Critical Review* 14/4 (2000): 441–58.

143 John Gray, *Two Faces of Liberalism*, p. 20.

144 Alan Ryan, 'Live and Let Live'.

145 See, for example, Yves Charles Zarka, *Hobbes et la pensée politique moderne*, Paris: PUF, 1995.

146 Charles Larmore, *The Morals of Modernity*, p. 164.

Chapter 3 Reconciliation and Public Reason

1   John Rawls, *Collected Papers*, pp. 1–19.
2   John Rawls, *Lectures on the History of Political Philosophy*. Cambridge, MA: Harvard University Press, 2007, p. 313.
3   John Rawls, *Collected Papers*, pp. 616–22.
4   John Rawls, *Lectures on the History of Political Philosophy*, p. 7.
5   John Rawls, *Political Liberalism*, p. 134.
6   Ibid., p. xviii.
7   Robert B. Talisse, 'Liberalism, Pluralism, and Political Justification', *The Harvard Review of Philosophy* 13/2 (2005): 59.
8   Robert B. Talisse, *Democracy after Liberalism*. London: Routledge, 2005, p. 9.
9   Russell Muirhead and Nancy L. Rosenblum, 'Political Liberalism vs "The Great Game of Politics": The Politics of Political Liberalism', *Perspectives on Politics* 4/1 (2006): 106.
10 John Rawls, 'Outline of a Decision Procedure for Ethics', in his *Collected Papers*. This essay was first published in 1951.
11 John Rawls, *Collected Papers*, p. 421.
12 Sheldon S. Wolin, *Politics and Vision*. Princeton, NJ: Princeton University Press, 2004, p. 533.
13 John Rawls, *Political Liberalism*. New York: Columbia University Press, 1996, p. 101.
14 Anthony Simon Laden, 'The House That Jack Built: Thirty Years of Reading Rawls', *Ethics* 113 (2003): 387–9.
15 John Rawls, *A Theory of Justice* (revsd edn), p. 393.
16 John Rawls, *The Law of Peoples*. Cambridge, MA: Harvard University Press, 1999, p. 11.
17 Jean-Jacques Rousseau, *The Social Contract and Other Later Political Writings*. Cambridge: Cambridge University Press, 1997, p. 41. Quoted by Rawls in his *The Law of Peoples*, p. 7.
18 John Rawls, *The Law of Peoples*, p. 7.
19 John Rawls, *Lectures on the History of Political Philosophy*, p. 239.
20 Thomas Nagel, *Equality and Partiality*. New York: Oxford University Press, 1991, p. 21.
21 Thomas Nagel, *Equality and Partiality*, p. 22.
22 Sheldon S. Wolin, 'The Liberal/Democratic Divide. On Rawls's *Political Liberalism*', *Political Theory* 24/1 (1996): 117.
23 John Rawls, *Political Liberalism*, p. 44.
24 Isaiah Berlin, 'Does Political Theory Still Exist?', in *Concepts and Categories*.
25 John Rawls, *Political Liberalism*, p. 46.
26 Bernard Williams, *In the Beginning was the Deed*, p. 2.

27 John Rawls, *Justice as Fairness*, p. 4, footnote.

28 John Rawls, *Lectures on the History of Political Philosophy*, p. 11.

29 John Rawls, *Justice as Fairness*, p. 33.

30 John Rawls, *Justice as Fairness*, pp. 35–6. See also *Political Liberalism*, pp. 54–8.

31 David A. Reidy, 'Reciprocity and Reasonable Disagreement: From Liberal to Democratic Legitimacy', *Philosophical Studies* (2007): 243–91.

32 John Rawls, *Justice as Fairness*, p. 36.

33 George Klosko, 'Political Constructivism in Rawls's *Political Liberalism*', *American Political Science Review* 91/3 (1997): 635–46.

34 Charles Larmore, *The Morals of Modernity*, p. 151.

35 Jacques Ranciere, *Disagreement*. Minneapolis, MN: University of Minnesota Press, 1999.

36 Charles Larmore, *The Morals of Modernity*, p. 171.

37 William A. Galston, *Liberal Pluralism*, pp. 44–7.

38 Robert B. Talisse, 'Rawls on Pluralism and Stability', *Critical Review* 15/1–2 (2003): 178.

39 A clear example is Stuart Hampshire, 'Liberalism: The New Twist', *New York Review of Books* (12 August 1993): 43–7.

40 J. Raz, 'Facing Diversity: The Case of Epistemic Abstinence', *Philosophy and Public Affairs* 19 (1990): 3–46.

41 John Rawls, *Political Liberalism*. p. xxv.

42 Charles Larmore, *Patterns of Moral Complexity*. Cambridge: Cambridge University Press, 1987, p. 73.

43 I have taken this term from Judith Shklar, 'The Liberalism of Fear', in Nancy Rosenblum (ed.), *Liberalism and the Moral Life*. Cambridge, MA: Harvard University Press, 1989, pp. 21–38. Shklar, in fact, denies the 'metapolitical assumption' that liberalism must rest upon a doctrine of pluralism of the kind proposed by Isaiah Berlin.

44 John Rawls, *Political Liberalism*, p. 37; 'The Domain of the Political', p. 235.

45 John Rawls, 'The Domain of the Political', p. 235.

46 John Rawls, 'Introduction to the Paperback Edition', *Political Liberalism*, p. xl.

47 John Rawls, *Political Liberalism*, p. xx.

48 Charles Larmore, *The Morals of Modernity*, p. 151.

49 John Rawls, *Justice as Fairness*, pp. 89–94.

50 Charles Larmore, 'Public Reason', in Samuel Freeman (ed.), *The Cambridge Companion to Rawls*. Cambridge: Cambridge University Press, 2003, p. 368.

51 For example, Brian Barry, 'John Rawls and the Search for Stability', *Ethics* 105/4 (1995): 874–915; Brian Barry, *Justice as Impartiality*. Oxford: Clarendon Press, 1995.

52 Peter Berkowitz, 'The Ambiguities of Rawls's Influence', *Perspectives on Politics* 4/1 (2006): 124.

53 Sheldon S. Wolin, 'The Liberal/Democratic Divide. On Rawls's *Political Liberalism*', *Political Theory* 24/1 (1996): 103.

54 John Rawls, *Justice as Fairness*, p. 118.

55 Bernard Williams, *In the Beginning was the Deed*, p. 2.

56 John Rawls, *Political Liberalism*, p. 136.

57 John Rawls, *Collected Papers*, p. 483.

58 Stuart Hampshire, 'Liberalism: The New Twist', *New York Review of Books*, 12 August 1993, p, 44,

59 John Rawls, 'Public Reason', p, 766,

60 Ibid., p. 766.

61 Joseph Raz, 'Facing Diversity: The Case for Epistemic Abstinence', *Philosophy and Public Affairs* 19/1 (1990): 7.

62 Ibid., p. 771.

63 Ibid., p. 807.

64 Ibid., p. 807.

65 Ibid., p. 766.

66 John Rawls, Introduction to the paperback edition of *Political Liberalism*. New York: Columbia University Press, 1995, p. lxi.

67 John Rawls, 'The Idea of Public Reason', p. 765.

68 John Rawls, 'The idea of Public Reason', p. 765.

69 John Rawls, *Political Liberalism*, pp. 212–13.

70 Ibid., p. 213.

71 Ibid., *Political Liberalism*, p. 214.

72 John Rawls, 'The Idea of Public Reason', p. 769.

73 John Rawls, 'The Idea of Public Reason Revisited', p. 581 (*Collected Papers*).

74 John Rawls, 'The Idea of Public Reason', p. 770.

75 Ibid., p. 771.

76 John Rawls, *Political Liberalism*, p. 175.

77 Ibid., p. 375.

78 John Rawls, 'The Idea of Public Reason', p. 578.

79 John Rawls, *Political Liberalism*, p. 250.

80 András Körösényi, 'Political Representation in Leader Democracy', *Government and Opposition* 40/3 (2005): 358–78.

81 John Rawls, *Political Liberalism*, p. 254.

82 Ibid., p. 251.

83 Ibid., p. 252.

84 Peter Berkowitz, 'The Ambiguities of Rawls's Influence', *Perspectives on Politics* 4/1 (2006): 123.

85   John Rawls, *Political Liberalism*, p. xlix.
86   Charles Larmore, 'Public Reason', in *The Cambridge Companion to Rawls*, p. 388.
87   For a critical account in these terms, see Steven Lukes, 'Of Gods and Demons: Habermas and Practical Reason', in J. B. Thompson and D. Held (eds), *Habermas: Critical Debates*. London: Macmillan, 1982, pp. 134–48.
88   Jürgen Habermas, *Legitimation Crisis*. London: Heinemann, 1976, p. 95.
89   Peter Dews (ed.), *Habermas: Autonomy and Solidarity*. London: Verso, 1986, p. 206.
90   Jürgen Habermas, *Legitimation*, p. 97.
91   Ibid., p. 106.
92   Ibid., p. 111.
93   Ibid., p. 107.
94   John Rawls, *Political Liberalism*, p. 374.
95   Jürgen Habermas, *The Inclusion of the Other: Studies in Political Theory*. Cambridge, MA: MIT Press, 1998, p. 49.
96   Ibid., p. 77.
97   Ibid., p. 73.
98   Ibid., p. 79.
99   Ibid., pp. 80–1.
100 Ibid., p. 94.
101 Ibid., p. 96.
102 See, for example, John Rawls, *Political Liberalism*, pp. 8–9.
103 Jürgen Habermas, *The Inclusion of the Other*, p. 97.
104 Ibid., p. 98.
105 Ibid., p. 99.
106 Ibid., p. 66.
107 Ibid., p. 101.
108 John Rawls, *Political Liberalism*, p. 373.
109 Ibid., p. 374.
110 Ibid., p. 378.
111 Ibid., pp. 378–9.
112 Jürgen Habermas, *The Inclusion of the Other*, p. 76.
113 Hilary Putnam, *The Collapse of the Fact/Value Dichotomy*. Cambridge, MA: Harvard University Press, 2002, pp. 111–34.
114 Ibid., p. 3.
115 Ibid., p. 112.
116 Jürgen Habermas, *Truth and Justification*. Cambridge: Polity, 2003, p. 235.
117 Ibid., p. 233.
118 See the remarks of Samantha Basson, *The Morality of Conflict*, p. 37. On this division, see Habermas, *Between Facts and Norms*. Cambridge: Polity, 1996.

119   Charles Larmore, *The Morals of Modernity*, p. 205.
120   Quentin Skinner, 'Habermas's Reformation', *The New York Review of Books* 29/ 15 (1982).
121   Sheldon S. Wolin, *Politics and Vision: Expanded Edition*. Princeton, NJ: Princeton University Press, 2004, p. 540, describes Rawls's 'genealogy of liberalism'. See also Jan-Werner Müller, 'Rawls, Historian: Remarks on Political Liberalism's "Historicism"', *Revue Internationale de Philosophie* 60 (2006): 327–39.
122   Bernard Williams, *In the Beginning was the Deed*, p. 53.
123   John Rawls, *The Law of Peoples*, p. 124.
124   Brian Barry, 'Political Theory, Old and New', in Robert E. Goodin and Hans-Dieter Klingemann (eds), *A New Handbook of Political Science*. Oxford: Oxford University Press, 1996, p. 538; this point is made by Müller, see n. 121 above.
125   Pierre Manent, *An Intellectual History of Liberalism*. Princeton, NJ: Princeton University Press, 1994, p. 78.
126   David Dyzenhaus, *Legality and Legitimacy*. Oxford: Clarendon Press, 1997, p. 221.
127   John Rawls, *Political Liberalism*, p. xxiv.
128   Bernard Williams, *In the Beginning was the Deed*, p. 2.
129   Sheldon S. Wolin, *Politics and Vision*, p. 540.
130   D. Dyzenhaus, *Legality and Legitimacy*. Oxford: Clarendon Press, 1997, p. 221.
131   John Rawls, *Political Liberalism*, p. xxvlll (Introduction to the paperback edition).
132   Catherine Audard, 'John Rawls (1921–2002). Presentation', *Revue Internationale de Philosophie* 3 (2006): 282.
133   Sheldon S. Wolin, 'The Liberal/Democratic Divide: On John Rawls's *Political Liberalism*', *Political Theory* 24/1 (1996): 116.
134   John Rawls, *Political Liberalism*, p. lxii; Peter de Marneffe, 'The Problem of Evil, the Social Contract, and the History of Ethics', *Pacific Philosophical Quarterly* 82 (2001): 11–25.
135   John Rawls, *Political Liberalism*, p. lxii (Introduction to the paperback edition).
136   John Rawls, *Political Liberalism*, p. 175.
137   Susan Neiman, *Evil in Modern Thought*. Princeton, NJ: Princeton University Press, 2002, pp. 310–14.
138   John Rawls, *The Law of Peoples*, p. 124.
139   John Rawls, *Justice as Fairness*, p. 3; *The Law of Peoples*, pp. 126–7.
140   Stephen B. Smih, 'The Philosopher of Our Times', *The New York Sun*, 11 May 2007.
141   John Rawls, *Justice as Fairness*, p. 121.
142   Rawls uses this phrase in *Justice as Fairness*, p. 115.

143 Stephen B. Smith, 'The Philosopher of Our Times', *New York Sun* (11 May 2007), online.
144 John Rawls, *Lectures on the History of Political Philosophy*, pp. 23–99.
145 John Rawls, *Justice as Fairness*, p. 1.
146 John Rawls, *Lectures on the History of Political Philosophy*, p. 10; *Justice as Fairness*, p. 3.
147 Raymond Geuss, *Outside Ethics*, pp. 38–9.
148 Christian Arnsperger, 'What is Utopian about the Realistic Utopia? Relocating Rawls in the Space of Normative Proposals', *Revue Internationale de Philosophie* 3 (2006): 295.
149 John Rawls, *Justice as Fairness*, p. 139.
150 Jan-Werner Müller, 'Rawls, Historian: Remarks on Political Liberalism's "Historicism"', *Revue Internationale de Philosophie* 60 (2006): 336.
151 John Rawls, *The Law of Peoples*, p. 128.
152 Ibid., p. 123.
153 Raymond Geuss, *Outside Ethics*, p. 16.
154 John Rawls, *Collected Papers*, p. 616.
155 John Rawls, *Lectures on the History of Moral Philosophy*. Cambridge, MA: Harvard University Press, 2000, pp. 160–1; Peter Berkowitz, 'The Ambiguities of Rawls's Influence', *Perspectives on Politics* 4/1 (2006): 121–33.
156 Rawls indicates his affinity with Judith Shklar's 'liberalism of fear' in *Political Liberalism*, p. 374.

Chapter 4 Pluralism: Reconciliation and Disagreement

1 Peter Bauman and Monika Betzler (eds), *Practical Conflicts*. Cambridge: Cambridge University Press, 2004.
2 Raymond Geuss, *Outside Ethics*, p. 31
3 Raymond Geuss, *History and Illusion in Politics*. Cambridge: Cambridge University Press, 2001, p. 156.
4 This is the view of Max Weber in his essay '"Objectivity" in Social Science and Social Policy', in Weber, *The Methodology of the Social Sciences*. This point is made well by Raymond Geuss, *Philosophy and Real Politics*. Princeton, NJ: Princeton University Press, 2008, pp. 1–23.
5 Bernard Williams, *In the Beginning was the Deed*.
6 Thomas Nagel, *Equality and Partiality*, p. 6.
7 Marc Stears, 'Liberalism and the Politics of Compulsion', *British Journal of Political Science* 37 (2007): 533–53.
8 Raymond Geuss, *Outside Ethics*, p. 19.

9   Raymond Geuss, *Public Goods, Private Goods*. Princeton, NJ: Princeton University Press, 2001, pp. 94–5, 100–2.
10 Isaiah Berlin, *The Crooked Timber of Humanity*, p. 15.
11 Glyn Morgan, 'The Realism of Raymond Geuss', *Government and Opposition*, 2005, pp.110–20.
12 Bernard Yack, 'Rhetoric and Public Reasoning', *Political Theory* 34/4 (2006): 434
13 C. A. J. Coady, *Messy Morality. The Challenge of Politics*. Oxford: Clarendon Press, 2008, p. 11.
14 Glen Newey, *After Politics*. Basingstoke: Palgrave, 2001; Bonnie Honig, *Political Theory and the Displacement of Politics*. Ithaca, NY: Cornell University Press, 1993.
15 Samantha Besson, *The Morality of Conflict*, esp. pp. 1–7.
16 Bernard Williams, *In the Beginning was the Deed*, p. 13.
17 Joseph Raz, 'Disagreement in Politics', *The American Journal of Jurisprudence* 43 (1998): 25.
18 Ruth Chang (ed.), *Incommensurability, Incomparability, and Practical Reason*.
19 Bernard Williams, *In the Beginning was the Deed*, p. 77.
20 Alasdair MacIntyre, 'Does Applied Ethics Rest on a Mistake?', *The Monist* 67 (1984): 498–513.
21 Aurel Kolnai, 'The Moral Theme in Political Division', *Philosophy* 35 (1960): 234.
22 Judith Shklar, *Ordinary Vices*. Cambridge, MA: Harvard University Press, 1984, pp. 226–49.
23 Jacques Rancière, *On the Shores of Politics*. London: Verso, 2007, p. 13.
24 Maurizio Viroli, *From Politics to Reason of State*. Cambridge: Cambridge University Press, 1992.
25 Ibid., p. 281.
26 Hannah Arendt, *The Human Condition*; Pierre Manent, *A World beyond Politics?*
27 Jeremy Waldron, *Law and Disagreement*, p. 3.
28 Dana Villa, *Socratic Citizenship*. Princeton, NJ: Princeton University Press, 2001, p. 297.
29 Amy Gutmann and Dennis Thompson, *Democracy and Disagreement*. Cambridge, MA: Harvard University Press, 1996, p. 21.
30 Ibid., p. 22.
31 Ibid., p. 25.
32 Jeremy Waldron, *The Dignity of Legislation*, pp. 153–4.
33 Jeremy Waldron, *Law and Disagreement*, p. 102.
34 Ibid., p. 112.
35 Ibid., p. 154.

36 Ibid., p.156.
37 Ibid., p. 229.
38 Ibid., p. 295.
39 David Estlund, 'Jeremy Waldron on Law and Disagreement', *Philosophical Studies* 99 (2000): 111–28.
40 Jeremy Waldron, *The Dignity of Legislation*, pp. 153–4.
41 William A. Galston, 'Democracy and Value Pluralism', *Social Philosophy and Policy* 17/1 (2000): 255.
42 Jeremy Waldron, *The Dignity of Legislation*, p. 152.
43 Michael Walzer, 'Deliberation, and What Else?', in Stephen Macedo (ed.), *Deliberative Politics*. New York: Oxford University Press, 1999, pp. 58–69.
44 Cheryl Misak, *Truth, Politics, and Morality*. London: Routledge, 2000.
45 Ibid., p. 128.
46 Ibid., pp. 9–10.
47 Raymond Geuss, *History and Illusion in Politics*, p. 155.
48 Cheryl Misak, *Truth, Politics, and Morality*, p. 131.
49 David Wiggins, *Needs, Values, Truth*, p. 343.
50 John Rawls, *Justice as Fairness*, p. 5.
51 Bernard Williams, *In the Beginning was the Deed*, p. 2.
52 Bernard Williams, 'Political Philosophy and the Analytic Tradition', in M. Richter (ed.), *Political Theory and Political Education*. Princeton, NJ: Princeton University Press, 1980, p. 67.
53 John Rawls, *A Theory of Justice*, p. 46.
54 Paul Kelly, *Liberalism*. Cambridge: Polity, 2005, p. 94.
55 Chantal Mouffe, *The Return of the Political*, p. 2.
56 Paul Kelly, *Liberalism*, p. 109.
57 Bernard Williams, *In the Beginning was the Deed*, pp .76–8.
58 This point is made by Jeremy Waldron in *Law and Disagreement*, p. 159.
59 Jeremy Waldron, *Law and Disagreement*, p. 229.
60 Thomas Hobbes, *Leviathan*. Indianapolis, IN: Hackett, 1994), pp. 243–4.
61 John Gray, *Two Faces of Liberalism*, p. 139.

Index

Information Commons
Level 0

Customer name: Barshagul Sakhypova
Customer ID: *******

Title: Global politics /
ID: 201094221
Due: 23/05/2016 23:59

Title: How to map arguments in political
science /
ID: 201026648
Due: 23/05/2016 23:59

Title: Pluralism /
ID: 201002994
Due: 23/05/2016 23:59

Total items: 3
15/05/2016 22:39

Thank you for using the Information Commons.

Problems with your library account?
Phone 0114 2227200 or email
library@sheffield.ac.uk